Children in the Worshiping Community

Children
in the Worshiping
Community

David Ng and Virginia Thomas

John Knox Press
ATLANTA

Library of Congress Cataloging in Publication Data

Ng, David.
    Children in the worshiping community.

    Bibliography: p.
    1. Worship (Religious education)   I. Thomas, Virginia,
1926-   . II. Title.
BV1522.N43   264   80-84655
ISBN 0-8042-1688-6   AACR2

To our partners in worship and in life,
Davis Thomas and Irene Ng

Preface

This book began in a summer workshop on children and worship. We two authors discovered that we had much in common concerning our sense of worship and our interest in including children in the life and worship of the church. One of us is a seminary professor who hopes to shape the ministry of worship leaders. One of us is a church school teacher who has sought to contribute to the education and worship of children in the local church. Both of us are convinced of the place of children in congregational worship. Together, that summer, we felt we had something to say about this important and timely topic.

But the genesis of this book lies beyond that initial summer meeting and decision to write. Our concerns and convictions are based on our individual experiences in worshiping communities. Though we now stand on common ground our travel to this destination was over different routes. Each of us must speak first as an individual of our acknowledgments and then as a team.

Worship for me began at home. I learned to worship the way I learned to speak—by living with two persons who worshiped. Their example was reinforced by deliberate education. I was blessed by experiences of learning hymns around the piano; reading from the Bible and hymnbook; "homegrown" worship services when illness or travel kept my family from the gathered congregation; talking about sermons, sacraments, and "the chief end of man"; making a pledge of money and talents; and placing my offering in my envelope on Saturday night. In acknowledging contributions to this book I must thank my parents, Paul and Vesta Coffin.

I have grown in worship as I have worshiped with children. The observations and questions of Nancy, Ann, Martha,

Dave, and Mark, and then through the years the questions and observations of dozens of young companions in worship, have kept me honest, awake, and involved.

For over three decades now I have been sustained in worship by ministerial leadership of theological integrity and pastoral concern. Happily free of any "star" mentality, Davis Thomas has assumed that each member of the congregation has a contribution to make in worship and that "congregation" means both children and adults. The primary factor in my continued efforts to interpret worship to children and children to adults has been this attitude.

David Ng's generous invitation to write and teach with him has enabled me to organize and present ideas and experiences in a way I would never have attempted alone. His knowledge, skill in teaching, and friendship have been generously shared in the team effort.

Worship for me began with a caring, supportive, nurturing community of faith: the Presbyterian Church in Chinatown, San Francisco. In this church, life and liturgy blended together. Daily events took meaning from the profound truths demonstrated at the Lord's Table. Life was seen as holy, love was expressed through fellowship, and mission was accepted as the natural outcome of having worshiped together. I was supported by the community in worship, was given opportunities to reflect upon my experiences, and even now feel a spiritual communion with the saints in my home church wherever and whenever I worship. My appreciation for the inclusiveness of communion, as well as its aspects of joy and eucharist, began with my participation in the sharing of bread and wine with brothers and sisters in Christ at a table in a ghetto church.

In recent years my association with church educators, pastors, and seminary students has fostered a desire to apply my experiences and understandings of worship to the special area of the church's ministry with children. In trying to help a seminarian, Don Cameron, with his doctoral project I was immensely helped. And when I found, during my attempts to teach a workshop on worship with children, someone who had been doing many sensible and wonderful things with children to enable them to worship, I knew that she and I could form a partnership to write a useful book. I'm grateful to Virginia Thomas for that partnership.

Together we gratefully acknowledge the many persons who have participated in workshops and have shared ideas, questions, and insights with us. We are indebted to Walter Funk of Austin, Texas, and Davis Thomas of New Port Richey, Florida, for the excerpts from sermons they have preached which are quoted in this book. We thank the faculty of Austin Presbyterian Theological Seminary for their constructive criticism of a monograph on children and worship, the ideas of which have been incorporated into this book. Special thanks go to Irene Ng for typing many, many pages of manuscript accurately, quickly, and usually cheerfully.

Virginia Thomas
David Ng

Contents

1 Children and Worship: Problems and Possibilities

It is 10:55 on Sunday morning. On the steps of the church sanctuary a full scale rebellion is in progress. Eight-year-old Laura North faces her parents defiantly and says, "But *why* do I have to go to church? I want to go home with Anita. We're going to cook out and swim in their pool. They're not staying for church, why do I have to?"

A Cluster of Questions

You have probably heard this question phrased in several different ways. You may even have tried to answer it.

When a child's cherished plans are thwarted and the words are an angry challenge, you may have pursued the fruitless task of explaining the worship encounter concealed by that inadequate phrase, "going to church." Or you may have retreated to the ultimate refuge of adult authority: "Because I said so."

A concerned parent may have expressed the matter to you differently: "Don't you think the church service is too long for a child Adrian's age? He doesn't get anything out of the sermon."

Perhaps as a teacher you have faced the questions positively. What is the meaning of worship with the congregation to a child? How can he or she enter this experience?

Or because you are responsible for planning and leading the worship of the church you have asked the question yourself. What do we do with children of preschool and elementary school age during the worship service on Sunday morning?

However you have come to ask and answer the questions, thinking about children and worship raises a host of related questions. What do we believe about the church and children's place in it? What do we believe about worship? How are we to worship God and how can we lead all persons effectively in worship?

Questions from the World

While we ask these questions from within the church, the society in which we worship raises some searching questions about children and corporate worship as well.

Choosing to worship regularly with our children and other Christians today calls for a disciplined commitment. There is nothing sacred about gathering at 11:00 A.M. each Sunday. (This is an hour chosen by rural America to fall midway between the hours for milking.) Any day or time may be holy; varied times for worship are a necessity in a land of such diverse working schedules. When we choose to worship is not so much the question as the choice itself in a culture which neither supports nor understands the act.

Our society is divided into age groups. Children are in school or child care centers with peers; parents work with other adults; senior citizens live in retirement centers. Why should children participate in an intergenerational experience of worship?

Families are fragmented. Divorce, conflicting work schedules, and the easy invitation of television entertainment make relationships a hard won achievement. Can we justify relating to the household of God in worship?

Businesses are open as usual on Sunday. Shopping, sports events, and a variety of community activities compete with almost any hour for worship. Is a holy day and hour reasonable in a secular culture?

Religious broadcasting offers music, prayer, sermons, and

salvation to a stay-at-home audience. Why should children or adults leave the comfort of living room to gather in a special place?

Children learn today in ways that are varied, active, and appropriate to their ages and capabilities. Educational psychology and television have combined to make education and entertainment synonymous. Is the distance between "Sesame Street" and the church's liturgy too great for children to bridge?

Within the church worship is considered optional. Almost half of those who claim church membership are absent each Sunday. The world without and within the church challenges our call to children to corporate worship. We need to give answers with clarity and conviction.

A Question of Obedience

We follow a Lord who placed children "in the midst of them" (Mark 9:36). Jesus himself came into the world as a baby and grew as a child. He welcomed and blessed children when his friends thought them an interruption. He used a child to illustrate the attitudes necessary for entrance into his kingdom. The smallest ministry to a child was service to him. He pronounced the most damning judgment on those who caused children to stumble. The last week of his life he treasured their song as "perfect praise" (Matt. 21:16).

Throughout history the church has tried, often imperfectly, to follow the example of Christ's attitude toward children. The early church opposed abortion and the exposure of unwanted infants. Hospitals, schools, and orphanages developed as the church's means of caring for children. Christian leaders led the fight to protect children from exploitation in the industrial revolution.

Obedience to Christ demands a peculiar concern for children among us. It would be ironic indeed if we consider the welfare of children in every area except that most central point in our life—worship.

Searching for Answers

Where shall we find answers to our questions about children and congregational worship?

One place to begin is with the church's faith. A careful examination of our theology will help us understand our call to worship as God's people and the place of children in the church. In chapter 2 we will look at the theological rationale that answers the question, Why should children be included in corporate worship?

The study of child development offers answers from another perspective. Learning how children grow physically, mentally, and socially will give us clues to the needs and capabilities children bring to worship. Chapter 3 will help us explore what worship can mean to children. Later chapters will apply this theological and psychological knowledge in showing how children can be included.

Our own experiences with children as we praise, pray, and listen to God's Word can direct our quest for answers. Personal participation on these occasions may have precluded the detachment such observation requires. The following scenes are recorded to allow you to stand "outside" a worship service and see what happens.

The incidents are not fiction. Names have been changed to protect the innocent and events have been selected and edited. Still they all did occur much as they are presented here. And they all could occur on almost any Sunday in any church.

Scene I. The balcony of the sanctuary.

Larry, five and a half years old, arrives and takes his place on the front row. During the four minute prelude and invocation he—

        swings his feet,
        drops his church school leaflet and picture,
        picks both up,
        looks under the pew while on the floor,

uses the leaflet as a fan,
waves to Billy and his family with the leaflet,
waves to the Smiths who are smiling at him,
stands,
leans on the balcony rail,
identifies friends from the aerial view,
notices the contrast of bald heads and bouffant
     hairstyles,
contemplates the leaflet in his hand,
recalls Mother's reaction when the last leaflet was
     dropped,
resumes his seat,
holds his legs out stiffly,
crosses and uncrosses his legs several times,
strokes the velvet pew cushion, the wooden arm of the
     pew, and the rough texture of the hymnbook,
runs his finger along the sharp bulletin edge,
stands as the minister begins the invocation,
picks up the rhythm of the pulpit voice and drums it
     on the balcony rail,
shifts from one foot to the other, still keeping time,
glances at the ceiling,
studies the height, the play of the sun through the
     skylight, and the oak beams radiating from a central
     circle,
squints to test the effect,
lies down in the pew to get a better view of the
     ceiling,
kicks his brother in the process,
dodges his brother's retaliating kick,
moves over and stands again to make room for Mother
     who is changing places,
runs his finger along the inside of the book rack,
examines a ball of dust gleaned there,
returns to his study of the ceiling,
holds his hand up to see the contrast of distant space
     and light,
stretches higher, still higher, still. . .

Larry's mother, assisting him from the floor with less than gentle hands, says through clenched teeth, "Be still! Be quiet! Be good!"

Scene II. Downstairs on the back row. The first hymn has just ended.

Six-year-old Jan is suddenly aware of the hymnbook.

"Hey!" she exclaims, "I know this word. It's b-o-o-k. Book."

"SHHHH-hhhh," cautions her older sister audibly.

"What does h-y-m-" begins Jan. Her sister instantly interrupts. "It's hymn. Hymnbook. Shhh."

Jan takes a pencil from her sister's purse and prints the word carefully on the bulletin and displays it proudly to those around her. Her sister praises the neat printing and marks "A-plus" beside it.

Now Jan, with the intensity of one who has discovered a vocation, continues through the hymnbook copying every word she recognizes on the bulletin margins. When this space is exhausted, she moves on to debt retirement envelopes and fellowship cards from the pew rack. She shares each accomplishment with her sister.

Mr. Downs, seated in front of the girls, adjusts his hearing aid while indignant, unspoken questions rattle in his mind and shape his facial expressions: Why do children come to church when they don't behave? Why can't they pay attention? Why are they here without their parents? Why are they so destructive, wasting cards and envelopes that way? Why can't they be quiet?

Scene III. The choir loft.

The Junior Choir, resplendent in new purple stoles for Lent, has just completed a well-sung anthem. John Fong, the minister, reads the story of the feeding of the five thousand.

Joe, an alert fifth grader, engages in the following mental monologue during the scripture: I know that story. I painted that picture for our mural downstairs. I didn't get five thousand people on the page though. How did they know that many were there? Did somebody count them? I don't like fish that much. I wonder what they did with all that leftover food?

Joe now reads the sermon title in the bulletin. "The Compassionate Vision" does not speak to his immediate concern, and the opening sentence of the sermon confirms this.

Dr. Fong says, "Spiritual myopia is a universal affliction that is particularly deplorable in the followers of one whose compassionate vision saw the multitude and penetrated beyond (etc.)."

Joe continues his mental comments: Twenty/twenty vision was on a TV program. It's good. Do I have it? I can see to the back row. Why is that man wearing dark glasses in church? I can count eight people wearing glasses.

Some of Dr. Fong's words do address Joe's interest for he hears: "Christ's vision in us, like a telescope, brings distant suffering into. . ."

Telescope. Daddy said no airplanes or rockets from the bulletin, but he didn't say anything about telescopes, thinks Joe. So he proceeds to roll the bulletin into a telescope, training it first on the congregation, then the windows, then Dr. Fong.

Further possibilities come to Joe's creative mind. Two bulletins could become binoculars. He turns to his neighbor, Paul. Through a noticeable rattle of papers Paul is heard saying, "I need it. It's mine."

The idea of telescope making is transmitted through the choir like a contagious disease. Twelve telescope-bulletins appear behind the choir rail. These are visible to the congregation and to Dr. Fong when the reaction of his listeners causes him to glance over his shoulder. The choir director intervenes and the telescopes disappear. Dr. Fong hurries on to point three and an "Amen."

The minister's meditation during the offertory is something like this: I'm not sure having children sing in worship is such a good idea. It may be too stimulating for them. It's hard enough to stir this group of adults to feed the hungry. How can I be expected to speak to children, too?

Scene IV. The time of the offering.

Sally, age seven, waits with keen anticipation as the ushers move down the aisle. She hums and clicks together two quarters left by the tooth fairy. At the last possible moment she seals the quarters in a red envelope marked "World Hunger."

Mrs. Lenz, seated on Sally's right, places her offering in the plate and attempts to pass it over Sally's head. Sally intercepts the offering plate and places it in her lap. She makes a small nest among the bills, envelopes, and change and places all her worldly goods in the center with reverent deliberation.

"Sally, you're making everyone wait," whispers her grandmother. "Hurry up. Here, let me. . ."

The clash and clatter of brass plate and coins furnishes a lively counterpoint for the offertory.

Scene V. The postlude.

As the assembled people of God disperse for the week we hear these comments:

Adult: Dr. Fong is a marvelous speaker! Such a rich vocabulary!

Child: Yuk! That was boring.

Adult: The music was inspiring.

Child: I liked it when we marched in singing loud. I knew all the words.

Adult: We must do something about world hunger.

Child: The offering plate made a funny sound. How much money was in it?

Adult: I felt the love and forgiveness of God.

Child: I got to sit with Billy and his family.

Adult: We had a good crowd today.

Child: There was more purple than anything—on the table, and the flowers, and the choir. But the preacher's socks were green.

Adult: The children were so restless it was almost impossible
to concentrate.
Child: I hate to sit still.

Children and Adults in Worship

Probably the scenes we have just witnessed were already
familiar to you. You may have been a major actor in such a
drama. You know what it is to feel responsible for a child's
behavior, what it is to be diverted or irritated by your own or
another's child. What we have seen may reinforce what we
have thought but never expressed. Children, adults, and congregational worship are unlikely partners.

When children and adults join together there are
problems. Children may bother adults and adults may restrict
children. Though they are present for a common event they do
not share a common experience.

Judging from the actions and responses of the young, they
seem to have gained little from the service. Some were repelled
by it, some uncomfortable in it, and some aware of the wrong
things, or aware of the right things for the wrong reasons.

We may take further note of the way children and adults
act and react. The energetic, active, observant children absorbed random experiences through every sense and pore.
The adults were engaged in selective verbal and mental activity. They valued order and ideas. They were present at
the service for a known reason and they did not wish to be
disturbed.

Some portions of the liturgy did engage children, and
some adults were concerned with superficial aspects of the
service. Yet on the whole we may decide that adults participated with understanding and benefit. Children did not.

Our initial answer to the question, What do we believe
about children and congregational worship? will probably be:
Worship is an experience for adults apart from children.

Because of the centrality of worship and because we count
our baptized children as part of the body of Christ, we are not

quite comfortable with our conclusion, but it seems to fit the facts.

No Deferred Answers

Even as we ponder our provisional answer, we are giving emphatic answers each time we gather as a church for worship. The way we involve or separate our children in our liturgy is a clear statement of belief about who we are and what we believe.

These next examples of children in worship will give us some grasp of the varied statements of faith we make each Sunday.

The Beth-Salem Church, 38 members, in a rural community.

John, two-and-a-half years old, and Catherine, four months old, came to worship with their parents. Catherine was asleep in her father's arms, and there were many offers to share his burden. There was a portable baby swing at the back of the sanctuary for Catherine in case she started to fuss.

John brought paper, crayons, a stuffed dog, and a blanket. He settled himself and his belongings along the pew beside his parents. He did not remain there long. He was free to sit beside anyone in his wandering, but he attracted no special attention. During the sermon and prayers he was treated with a kind of benign neglect—helped, hugged, or ignored without much fuss or concentration.

John joined in singing his version of the hymns and actually approximated the words of the Doxology. Once his hymn lasted longer than the congregation's. He copied the bowed heads in prayer for as long as five seconds. He stood by the end of the pew and placed his gift in the offering plate, then accompanied the usher to the front of the church.

At the close of the service John stood by the minister and shook hands with people for a few minutes, then joined two older children who rolled a ball with him while his parents visited. Catherine, now awake, was admired and held. About half the congregation went home to John's house for iced tea.

*Oceanside Church, 800 members, in a rapidly developing
retirement and resort community.*

It was Stewardship Sunday in Oceanside Church. Allan
and George, as usual, sat on the front row unattended. Their
father was at work and their mother sang in the choir. If today
was typical, they would be praised for their good behavior.

On this Sunday every person at church was given a pledge
card listing opportunities for service in the church and community. Rather, every adult was given a card. Allan and George
sat while others studied and filled out their pledges of talents.
When these were completed, each person brought the card to
the communion table.

Six-year-old George watched the process and began to fold
his picture from the church school into card size. He hurriedly
printed his name so he could join the procession to the table.

Allan, anxious to maintain their good reputation said,
"Don't do that. We're not supposed to have anything to give."

Greenville Church, 300 members, in an ordinary city of 20,000.

Kelly Miller, poised on the edge of her chair, watched her
choir director carefully. She had no bulletin (children rattle
them) so she was not quite sure when their anthem came in the
service. She had no hymnbook either (children drop them), but
she knew most of two hymns by memory. She stood and sang
the anthem with all the enthusiasm a seven-year-old could
muster. As she joined her parents in the congregation she was
satisfied and happy about her choir and her song.

When she slipped in beside her mother, Mrs. Lackey
leaned across Kelly to say to Mrs. Miller, "Aren't they cute? We
love it when the children sing."

*Trinity Church, downtown, the oldest church in town, 600
members and many visitors.*

The bulletin called it "Words for Young Christians." Dr.
McKinnon, aware of restless children and their limited understanding, invited them to come to the front of the sanctuary. It
made a break in the service adults welcomed and enjoyed. At

the same time the children liked the movement and special attention. They trekked happily to the area in front of the pulpit to meet with their friend.

It was Ari's first time in the church. At the age of nine he had curiosity and a desire to be a part of whatever was going on. He liked the challenge to learn that he usually encountered in the church. Though it was his first Sunday there, he joined the children and waited with interest.

"If you want to get to the top of the Empire State Building you will find there is a hard way and an easy way. Now what would be the hardest way to get to the top of such a tall building?" asked Dr. McKinnon.

"Jump," said Ari quickly.

Dr. McKinnon and the congregation laughed. "Climb the stairs" was the answer that fit the illustration of the two ways of life.

Ari returned to his seat and said to his father, "Let's don't come here again."

Peace Community Church, 160 members, in a small suburb.

Mr. Porter wanted to encourage families to bring their children to church. He liked children and he understood their need for concrete, everyday illustrations. He also wanted parents to be comfortable and enjoy the service with no interruptions. His plan was to keep the children as happy as possible during the first part of the service, then dismiss them for study and recreation after the junior sermon.

One representative Sunday Mr. Porter brought jelly beans and a scale to show the principle of God's measured judgment according to his perfect balances. (Mr. Porter always had a scripture verse as the basis for his talk.) In weighing the jelly beans, the minister spilled the entire bag of candy on the steps where the children sat.

"It's just like hitting the jackpot," exclaimed one child happily in the scramble to get his share of the candy. It proved an unforgettable sermon.

The University Church, 500 members, in a historic old city.

David watched from the balcony as his church school teacher was ordained.

"Next Sunday is an important day for me and for our church," she had told David and the kindergarten class the week before. "I've been chosen to be a special leader—an elder. It's a big responsibility and it's a little bit frightening. During the week I'll send you something to think about that will help you understand next Sunday's ordination."

David had received a paper called "Messages Without Words." It showed pictures of a smile, a handshake, a salute, and a bouquet of flowers. He was to watch the service to see an unspoken message and what it said.

After the service he met his teacher and told her, "I saw people put their hands on your head. I know what they were saying: Don't be scared. You get God's mighty hand!"

St. Timothy's Church, 1000 members, in an affluent suburb.

Bruce looked around the sanctuary with interest. Since his little sister was being baptized he was not attending Children's Church as usual. This was his first time to be in this room for any length of time. He gained a blurred impression of many faces, great distances, and a looming pulpit.

He described it without enthusiasm when he rejoined his friend who had been watching a movie about playing fair.

"It was O.K. The guy who talks put some water on her head. Then she got to go to her church. Mama and Daddy went to their church, and I got to go to mine. I like mine best."

The Church of the Covenant, 130 members, on the outskirts of a small city.

The school week had been shattered by a fight on the school bus. Racial tension had heightened. Parents threatened lawsuits. Classes were interrupted by arguments.

Before church school Leslie and Beth stopped by the

prayer box outside the minister's study. "Pray for our school" was written on the note they dropped in the box.

Mr. Wood had asked the fifth-grade class several months before about prayer. They had all confessed they seldom listened when he prayed so long on Sunday morning. The prayer box had been a result of that class meeting.

"Prayers of the people should be just that," Mr. Wood explained. "We need to help each other through our prayers and we need to pray together to God about what concerns us. God is interested in what eleven-year-old church members need, too."

As Mr. Wood asked the congregation to pray for their school that morning, Leslie and Beth felt somehow things would be better at school next week.

St. Andrew's Church, a new congregation meeting in a multipurpose room. About 175 members with many young families.

Cindy edged to the front of the circle of chairs so she could see everything. Her big brother and his junior high class were responsible for reading the scripture. She had heard him discuss the assignment from the first Sunday the project began.

The class had studied when the reading of scripture came in the order of worship and how the minister read it. Dr. Stussi had talked with them about the Word of God, how central it was in worship, and how preaching was built on it. The class finally decided that dramatizing was one way of "reading" so the Word would come to life.

The story was about Jesus healing the man with the withered hand on the sabbath. Cindy's brother was Jesus. There were also a narrator, the man with the withered hand, and angry Pharisees.

Cindy followed the reading with interest. Though she knew the story she held her breath when the Pharisees complained. The seventh graders had planned a dramatic pause here. Jesus could have refused or waited until another day.

Then Jesus told the man to come forward. Cindy clapped with pleasure even though the reading was not over, and in a few seconds the congregation joined in. Their joy in the healing provided a sharp contrast to the anger with which the Pharisees began to plot Jesus' death.

Conflicting Answers

What do we believe about children and their place in the worshiping household of God. Our answers are bewildering in their contradictions. Listen to some of them:

> Children are an important and loved part of this household.
> Children do not belong with us.
> Children are cute and entertaining.
> Children are capable of profound understanding.
> Children have nothing to give.
> Children can contribute and enrich our worship.
> Children bother us.
> Children's concerns are ours.

A brief review of our church scenes, from Larry's energetic actions to Cindy's final applause, shows why clear, consistent answers are difficult. Children and adults are different in ability and understanding. Corporate worship is a profound and demanding experience.

Still, when we see our attempts to resolve these problems we know how unsatisfactory some of our strategies are. With the best intentions we can exploit, isolate, demean, or ignore God's children.

On the other hand, children of many ages can be a part of the worship of God. In some scenes children were comfortable, involved, and knowledgeable. What caused the difference?

A broad understanding of worship was one source of difference. Formality was not confused with form, nor obscurity with profundity.

An understanding of children contributed to their meaningful worship. Their needs for physical care and comfort, for information, and for acceptance were met.

The Possibilities Within the Problem

Think once more of the children we have seen in worship. Recall Cindy's total absorption in and uninhibited response to the gospel, the dedicated work behind the junior high drama and the choir anthem, Sally's joy in giving and Sam's eagerness to take part. Listen to David's thoughtful definition of ordination and the school girls' request for prayer. Look at the visible symbol of a trusting child asleep and a toddler at home in the house of God.

Could what we often consider problems be assets? What could a child's awareness of the sanctuary and its symbols add to our worship? Could their motion and rhythm expand our understanding of worship beyond "sitting still"? What if their humor flavored our sobriety, their vocabulary limitations sharpened our communication, and their need for the concrete made visible our abstractions?

Children have certain abilities and attitudes which lie at the heart of worship. They are aware of their environment and the community around them. They are capable of intense identification and imaginative hearing. They are infectiously enthusiastic. They can be sacrificially generous and honest in their responses. They respond physically and emotionally to what they see and hear.

Adults have important abilities and attitudes as well. They have understanding and the perspective of experience and years. They can apply what is happening in the sanctuary to their life outside the sanctuary. They have the discipline to follow and direct their attention. They see the meaning behind the symbol, the relation of the parts to the whole. They have the words and forms to channel this corporate event.

A vital element in all ages worshiping together is this wedding of adult and childhood gifts in our corporate liturgy. Our differences become a rich harmony.

Because we love our children, because we follow Jesus, because we assume care for children in baptism, and because we are part of a covenant community that has always been called to teach its children, we ask searching questions about children and their place in corporate worship. We want them to worship God and we want to assume our responsibility for leading them intelligently.

Without changing our responsibility to teach, Jesus also called us to responsible learning. In a radical reversal of roles, the child became the teacher when Jesus "placed a child in the midst of them." We are called to learn from our children as well as to teach them.

Beyond the problems and tensions of all ages joined together lies the exciting opportunity to be the body of Christ. In a unique way we can use the gifts of each member to enrich the worship of all. We can develop a vital and enriching interplay between grown-ups and children in the presence of God. We can respond to our call to worship God with the voice of the whole people of God.

2 The Faith That Calls Children to Worship

The gospel is for all persons, regardless of age. The church includes persons of all ages. Worship is a corporate action in which children are participants with adults. These simple statements, developed in this chapter, form our theological basis for including children with the worshiping congregation. Following this chapter's presentation of theological concerns for children as members of the church and reasons for including them in congregational worship, succeeding chapters will show what children are capable of doing as they worship and how they can develop understandings and skills for worship.

Everyone Can Hear the Good News

Children belong with the worshiping congregation because the gospel is for persons of all ages. An adolescent seeks to form an identity. The gospel tells such a seeker that she is a child of God. One who is very old wonders about self-worth. The gospel answers the concern with assurance that God loves everyone, whether or not that one is working, has a family, has material possessions, or good health. Young adults await a vocation. The gospel says that one's talents are gifts from God, even as life itself is such a gift. Persons who have need for relationships and for community will be glad to hear that the gospel calls people out of loneliness and into community.

Human needs beckon especially loudly at certain times in a person's life. An adolescent's need for a sense of identity is such an example. But most needs occur and recur throughout life. Needs, like the need for food, are part of life throughout all of life. It is not only adults who have need for a sense of identity, or of self-worth, or for secure relationships and community. Children also have these needs. The gospel of God's love and redemption addresses the needs of adults, and the needs of children, too.

Particularly because they are so young and inexperienced and unlearned, children need a sense of belonging. They need to feel that they are a part of a loving group and that they not only will be cared for, but that they will be able to assert themselves, to respond to care, and even to return some caring themselves. Adults have these needs, too. Again, the gospel is inclusive, addressing the need to belong and to be a part of a caring group, as this need is felt by adults as well as children.

There is no minimum age requirement for hearing and receiving the gospel. Neither is there an age requirement for responding to it. Proper response to God's gift of love and relationship, if it can be measured at all, certainly is not judged by the sophistication of a reply, or the value of an offering, or the eloquence of a statement of faith. The response which is pleasing to God is simple trust. The ability to trust God, simply and wholeheartedly, is found in persons of all ages.

Everyone who hears and responds to the gospel can proclaim it, too. There are many ways to do this. Sometimes, however, in our concern for "proclaiming the gospel," we overlook the rich variety of ways in which the gospel may have come to us. The gospel is communicated not only through study classes but also through friendship. The love of Jesus Christ is as effectively made known by demonstration as by explanation. Some aspects of the gospel are best communicated by adults, with their intellectual maturity. Other aspects of this rich gospel may be effectively conveyed by young persons in ways that are winsome for their directness and lack of sophistication. Young and old are called to proclaim the gospel, and each age can do so with integrity and effectiveness.

The gospel is proclaimed with the greatest integrity and in word and deed by all ages together. All have contributions to make, and if one age group is missing, something is lost in the proclamation of the gospel. The gospel is demonstrated when all who have been touched by it join together as the household of God. By being a loving community of all kinds of persons the church witnesses to the love, acceptance, and care which is intended by the gospel.

Those who were called first to follow Jesus and to be his initial messengers of good news had to be reminded of the nature of the community they were to help establish. The kingdom of God was not to be without children. Children have a simple, trusting faith. Jesus wanted his disciples to show similar trust. There may be no more basic act in all of life than that of trusting God, and children can help us learn how to do it. "Whoever does not receive the kingdom of God like a child shall not enter it."(Mark 10:15).

Everyone Can Belong to the Body of Christ

Children belong with the worshiping congregation because the body of Christ has no age requirements. Christianity is age-inclusive. All who are baptized are members of the body of Christ. Children are members of the body—the church.

Over the years various New Testament pictures and descriptions of the church have been used to remind us that all church members are equally engaged in ministry. They remind us that we have tended to make a false dichotomy between laity and ordained clergy. But we also need to be confronted with the false dichotomy often created between children and adults in the church. Children and adults are equally members of the body of Christ. The gifts to the members and the demands placed upon them by the gospel are as true for children as they are for adults. Adults are to participate. Children are to participate. Adults are to contribute. Children are to contribute. Adults worship. Children worship.

How a member participates, contributes, and worships is influenced by who one is. Talents, circumstances, and, certainly, age affect a member's method and degree of participation in the church. But it is impossible to think of a member not participating—in one way or another.

What an adult church member does as a part of the life of the congregation is real and, it is hoped, has integrity. What a child who is a church member does as a part of the same congregation is equally real and, it is hoped, has equal integrity. Children can and do contribute to the life and ministry of the congregation. They do so simply by being present; the church would not be whole without children.

A happy trend in the church today is the growing awareness of the positive and useful contributions children can make to the life and ministry of the congregation. That children have a quality of faith we all can emulate has been mentioned. Adults can find that the simple trust in God expressed by children is not necessarily anti-intellectual and need not be a denial of the content of our faith. Simple trust is positive and useful precisely because it accepts the reality of that which is profound, mysterious, and cannot be known but must be believed.

Children are bearers of love and hope and grace. Sometimes parents are caught short by the realization that, in a special way, their child has brought the joy of the love of Christ into a life situation. Love, care, and nurture—ministry to one another—often is by embrace, by provocative questions, by laughter, by tears, and by simple deeds. Such ministry is often done by children.

A vivid way to realize the rightful place of children in the life and work of the church is to read aloud Romans, chapter 12. This message of encouragement and exhortation to the church is as meaningful for children as for any age group. Read the chapter with some children. Are they not also called to sacrificial living, to transformation by the renewal of their minds, to what is good and acceptable and perfect? Are they not also members of the body of Christ, with differing gifts? Can they not show faith and serve and teach and show mercy? Children can love, show honor, be aglow with the

Spirit, rejoice in hope, be patient in tribulation and constant in prayer. The church would not be whole without children.

Everyone Can Worship Together

Children belong with the worshiping congregation because worship is a corporate action. Concurrent with the rising interest in the role and contribution of children in the church is a growing understanding of worship. The church has endured a faddish contemporizing of worship, with its excesses of streamers, balloons, and superficial spontaneity and joy. However, a positive benefit from recent experimentation has been a recovery of the sense of worship as participation. One hoped-for result is a recovery of forms of worship with more congregational action. Another hoped-for result is the recovery of a broader interpretation of "congregation." In popular terms, the congregation is corporate and it is intergenerational. It includes young and old. In its life and worship the congregation includes children and adults.

A crucial aspect of worship which is being recovered today is the corporate nature of worship. Countering recent centuries of emphasis and overemphasis on individual religion and piety, the church, at least in significant part, is finding ways to express its corporate nature, especially as it worships together. The Bible can hardly be read without appreciation for faith and life in a corporate context. The Lord of history, the God of grace, was revealed to persons who were members of a covenant people. These people were called to mission and to worship as a people, not as individuals. Christian worship starts as corporate worship, engaged in by all who are members of the community of faith.

To understand the purposes and practices of Christian worship is to recognize the place of children in the worshiping community and the contributions that children bring to the corporate worship of the community.

A homespun illustration may point up the essentially corporate nature of our faith and our worship. A family is a corporate entity. Its togetherness is actualized in many ways but there is perhaps no more constant and enduring symbol of its corporateness than the family meal. The truism is that the family that eats together stays together! Certainly each member could eat individually, and at times must do so. And certainly many family meals include others, such as during a joyful celebration of a holiday. But the normative family meal is that of everyone in the family eating together. It is a corporate activity which contributes to and symbolizes the corporate nature of the family. Worship is for the household of faith a corporate activity—children and adults together—contributing to and symbolizing the unity of the household.

For the church to be whole children need to be included. Examples have already been given of how children contribute to the faith and life of the congregation. In similar ways they contribute to the worship of the whole congregation. Children bring to worship a directness and a simplicity of faith. They are spontaneous. They are receptive and have hope. They know how to show thankfulness and joy; indeed they show these feelings more wholly and wholeheartedly than do most adults. In many ways children enrich the worship of the church. Specific ways in which children enrich the worship will be evident throughout this book.

Alongside their contributions we can also list the needs of children, which can be met as they participate in worship. Each child, as a member of the church, needs opportunities to respond to God's gifts and God's calls. Worship is intended as a means of response, and children need to participate in the individual and collective responses. Prayers of praise, gifts of self, statements of belief, and songs of dedication are activities children need to practice, as do adults.

Whatever one's age, child and adult alike need to express the spiritual dimension of life and allow it to be nurtured. Every element of worship, including Word and sacraments, can provide that expression and that nurture. Further, children need to confess their sinfulness and be assured of pardon; they need to be inspired by hearing God's Word; they need to make public commitments of faith and intention. These are valid needs, but many churches deliberately or unwittingly prevent children, through exclusionary practices, from having these needs met.

Whatever worship could be or might be, it is usually designed to fit only the needs and interests of adults. Even when children are present at a service of worship they are ignored, and the worship activities are geared to adult styles of expression, or the children are subjects of condescension through token activities that are patently childish and inconsequential.

Worship does not have to be narrowly adult-oriented. Worship can have the depth of content and the integrity that reflect the highest of biblical and traditional standards and at the same time have appeal to children. If a congregation wishes to have corporate worship that is appropriate to children as well as adults, it can be done without resorting to gimmicks and distortions that are mistakenly thought to be appealing to children. Other sections of this book will offer specific suggestions and examples of how worship can be appropriate for everyone in the congregation, including children. The concern here is for an understanding that worship involves participation by everyone in the community of faith. The church seeks to say to the whole world that God's kingdom is for all, and that God's love draws all together. This can be said in the most visible of all church activities, its corporate worship. Children and adults worshiping together make this statement of faith.

Corporate worship at its best, engaged in by a faithful people with a profound sense of their identity as the community of faith, becomes the focal point for congregational life. Each Christian's life and the life of the community is mirrored in its worship. God initiates relationship; God calls persons to become a People; God forgives and redeems them; God teaches and nurtures them; God strengthens them for their daily tasks in the world created by God. So goes the pattern of Christian worship and so goes the pattern and rhythm of life itself. And we reiterate here that it is children and adults worshiping together that make worship and life parallel statements of faith. Without children life and worship would miss their childlikeness—spontaneity, simple trust, openness, and hope.

Corporate worship ought not to be confused with what might be called "spontaneous worship." The life of the community is structured by its worship together. And the personal, private, family, small group, and spontaneous worship of the faithful take their form from the basic corporate worship of the community. There is exquisite beauty in the way a child sees how some planted seeds have burst forth with leaf and bloom, and then exults, "Hurray, God, you did it!" The child's dance is sheer joy. It is valid worship and we all might be more faithful and responsive if we too would exult and dance. The practice of corporate worship might be enriched if some of the freedom to be spontaneous could be expressed. Perhaps children can help the church to be more free. What is disappointing, however, is that some churches convert and control spontaneity—they allow that children can be spontaneous in their worship and they allow children to practice such worship, but at times and places when adults are not present, certainly not when adults are gathered for corporate worship!

The church can be broad—it can encourage individuals to practice spontaneous or informal worship. Thanks can be given for food, prayers can be offered at bedtime, petitions can be voiced in times of fear or need. But such worship supplements corporate worship—it does not replace it. For all the opportunities that children or other groups of people may have for worship, we all, together, still need to participate in the basic activity that defines the church: [corporate worship.] Consider seriously a picture of an ideal service of worship which includes the participation of both children and adults.

> Worship in this ideal picture is framed by an ideal congregation which practices its sense of community and care for one another in all of its programs, from churchwide suppers to pastoral care by various members to social and educational activities that often are

done intergenerationally. Being together in worship is the highlight of being together at many other times in this congregation.

Worship in this congregation is no haphazard affair. Much planning, practice, and training prepares each worshiper. For example, new hymns are introduced at church suppers; responses are learned in church school; rituals and symbols are explained in bulletins, newsletters, and during the service. Opportunities are provided for parents of young children to learn about worship and about how to help their children to worship.

The service is as much traditional as it is contemporary. That is, the content of the service—the concepts and concerns of the prayers, songs, and sermon—are contemporary, but the form and many of the practices reflect worship that has been done in a similar manner since the formation of the church two thousand years ago and before that in the practices and forms of the Hebrew people. But the forms and practices are not lifeless. Rather, they are colorful, dramatic, symbolic, and they are very concrete, or tangible, and rich in imagery. While the children (and some adults) may not understand all the nuances of certain acts, they still find they can be caught up in participating in these acts. They stand up to praise God; they bow to meditate; they reach out and touch each other as they pass the peace; they recite together what they believe; they are reminded by art and color of the seasons and patterns of Christian devotional life; they gather, symbolically, at the Lord's Table to pray for one another and for all the saints in communion through Christ; they all say "Amen" together to indicate their active involvement in public prayer. These are but a few of the tangible ways the whole congregation praises God and is nurtured by God during worship.

Unless it is pointed out to the congregation, there is little notice of the pace and rhythm of the service of worship. The worship moves along with good pace, one act following another in good order. The order is logical and each element flows into the next, not just because of some tradition but because each element fits together to form a meaningful whole. No element seems out of place; apparently someone has taken care not to interject a practice that would intrude on the focus of worship which is the corporate praise of God.

There is no regular activity designed only for one age group—no children's sermon—and yet, even though there are many children and they stay for the whole service, they seem to be as interested and active in the worship as are the adults. Even during the sermon (seventeen minutes long) the children listen—to some of it—because they know that there are examples, images, stories, and points drawn from the situations and experiences of children as well as of adults.

This picture of worship may not seem ideal to some churches, for they are already practicing many of the activities described. This ideal picture, and many extensions and variations of it, are well within the reach of most congregations. This ideal picture only seeks to be faithful to what is already in our tradition.

Everyone Can See the Pictures of Grace

A widely accepted definition of the sacraments of baptism and communion is that these two rituals are signs and seals of God's grace. Most Christians understand the sacraments to be gifts of God that not only help us to recall God's mercy, but in a unique way become channels of grace. In baptism we acknowledge God's salvation and respond to it with thanksgiving and dedication. When infants are baptized the entire congregation acknowledges the child to be loved and claimed by God as a child of the covenant. The baptism, furthermore, is a way that the community promises to bring up the child to know and love God. The Lord's Supper is a rich sacrament with many meanings. It is a memorial, but much more than that. Participants in the Lord's Supper not only recall Christ's sacrifice and dedicate themselves as living sacrifices, but as they hear the Word and partake of the bread and wine they celebrate again the real presence of Christ in their midst. This gift of Christ's Spirit is a mystery we know to be true but cannot begin to explain—our best response is to receive this gift humbly and gratefully.

Basic to each sacrament is the element of faith. This is significant in our discussion of children and worship, because we must be mindful that the basis for participation in the sacraments is not knowledge but faith. The sacraments have their effect upon us more because we believe than because we can explain. This is as true for adults, with their store of knowledge and experience, as it is for children, with their lack of knowledge and experience because of their youth. The sacraments are for children as well as adults. At the core of the sacraments is a key characteristic: they are tangible signs and seals. Water, bread, and wine are materials which can be seen, touched, and tasted. That which is mysterious, by which we mean to say the wonder of God's grace, is communicated to people very tangibly through three common substances. Such directness and simplicity may surprise us. If so, to God be the glory. So thought John Calvin, when he wrote in the *Institutes of the Christian Religion:*

> The sacraments, therefore, are exercises which make us more certain of the trustworthiness of God's Word. And because we are of flesh, they are shown us under things of flesh, to instruct us according to our dull capacity, and to lead us by the hand as tutors lead children. Augustine calls a sacrament "a visible word" for the reason that it represents God's promises as painted in a picture and sets them before our sight, portrayed graphically and in the manner of images.[1]

The perceptions of Calvin and, before him, Augustine vivify for us the power of the sacraments to communicate. They are pictures, drawn by God, for our edification and nurture. Even when practiced by a congregation and a worship leader who are meager in their use of gesture and tone, the sacraments are moving, graphic, concrete, and dramatic. Of all the acts of corporate worship, the sacraments hold the most interest and appeal for children.

Reversing the trend of thinking that has characterized parts of the church, we can think in terms of the sacraments having special meaning and attraction for children! Children are recipients of God's grace. The sacraments are signs and seals of this truth. Children are quite correctly the "recipients" of the sacraments. Their membership in the covenant fellowship is sealed and sustained by water, bread, and wine.

Children are trusting persons. Trust is the attitude required of those who receive the water of baptism and the bread and wine of communion. This emphasis on trust, while it is in keeping with an appreciation of the mystery of the sacraments, has not been the common emphasis in the practice of some churches. Some churches have chosen to stress the proper discerning of the body of Christ—to ensure that those who partake of the bread and wine have a certain level of understanding of the meanings of the communion. Toward this end such churches have required communicant training, church approval, and confirmation prior to first communion. What makes this practice problematical is the suggestion that the efficacy of the sacrament rests upon right knowledge rather than upon trusting faith. To permit baptized children to partake of bread and wine is to acknowledge that God's grace is a gift, undeserved and received humbly and thankfully even though a full knowledge of the meaning of the sacrament has not been achieved.

To permit children to partake is to admit that beyond a general knowledge of the sacrament it can hardly be fair to expect children or adolescents to know about the mystery of the sacrament what adults in a lifetime may never come to know. We come to the Lord's Table because we trust God and have faith in God's mercy, not because we know how God's mercy operates.

When children partake of bread and wine the "tables are turned." Their participation in the sacrament of the Lord's Table teaches the rest of the church something very important about God and our relationship with God. We are prevented from a gnostic practice of our religion. The essence of gnostic religion is the right knowledge of certain secrets; thus is the path to salvation. The Lord's Supper and baptism are meant as gifts to be received in faith. We do not claim God's gifts through our superior intellect or knowledge of certain secrets kept from others. When children have the audacity to receive God's gifts, which they could in no way deserve on the basis of their knowledge or experience, the rest of the church can learn again the meaning of trust and faith. In the matter of a "right practice" of the sacraments, it is possible that the children shall lead us.

Properly speaking, we do not "observe" the sacraments, we "celebrate" them! We celebrate grace freely given, received by unworthy but grateful people. Baptism and communion are joyous, happy occasions. It could well be that children, who are good at celebrating, will lead us in our participation in the joyful feast.

3 The Children That Faith Calls to Worship

All of God's children have needs. For that matter, all persons, children and adults, have needs. This chapter focuses on children's needs, interests, and tasks which are a part of their natural development. Always keeping in mind that worship is a gift of God and a call from God to offer praise and thanks, we can consider how children grow, what they are capable of at each stage of growth, and how they can worship meaningfully and appropriately. After a review of social and mental development in children, examples will be given of how children in the several stages of development actually participate in worship.

Children Develop Socially

The description of the "eight ages of man" by Erik Erikson provides a useful framework for understanding how persons develop psychologically and socially from birth until death.[2] Basic to Erikson's schema is the idea that at each age of development a central issue arises to challenge the person. In dealing with the issue, often with the help of parents or others close to the person, that person may develop certain strengths which accrue to his or her personality and prepare that person to meet the issue that will arise in the next stage of development. The most familiar example of this phenomenon is the issue or "crisis" faced by adolescents: identity formation. Successful dealing with that crisis enables an adolescent, upon reaching young adulthood, to adequately face the new issue of how to establish intimate relationships.

Erikson points out that we all meet the challenges of each crisis to a greater or lesser degree. Sometimes we are very successful and can look forward to the next stage with confidence. Sometimes our resolution is rather negative and our failure hampers future development and will continue to do so until some way is found to resolve the crisis positively.

In Erikson's description of life, the first year of an infant's life presents that baby with the task or crisis of developing a sense of basic trust or basic mistrust. At this time the infant usually is shown love through cuddling, feeding, and the many other forms of care and tenderness. The infant is encouraged to form a view of self and of the world which is trusting. When one considers how much of religious life is founded upon trust, one can appreciate the significance of developing in one's first year of life a sense of basic trust. Experiences of extreme pain, lack of care, or physical or psychological cruelty or deprivation could lead to a sense of basic mistrust.

The years of early childhood, roughly fifteen months to two-and-one-half years of age, call for the development of a sense of autonomy, as opposed to a sense of shame and doubt. To be able to know oneself as an individual, with personal control over one's body, enhances the sense of autonomy. Not being able to exercise control and not being able to affect one's environment could cause the child to be ashamed and to doubt the worth of self and of the world. Such a devalued sense of self could emerge, for example, if a child cannot or will not gain control over body functions such as the processes of elimination.

In the next stage, at ages three to six, the child, usually while engaging in play, will develop either a sense of initiative or of guilt. If given opportunities to express one's thoughts through action, as when a child is allowed to use newly developed motor skills to cut with scissors or ride a tricycle, a sense of initiative comes about, along with its positive sense of ego. Not to be permitted such efforts, or to be criticized for poor achievement, is to create in the child a sense of guilt, a sense that one is not right and not acceptable.

To feel shame or guilt is to be faced with problems for which religion offers help. It is not only adults who sense that they are "not right" and are unacceptable. Children can sense this too. In whatever ways are appropriate children need to hear the good news that God is trustworthy, that God finds every person of great worth and accepts each one with love and relationship. One way this good news can be communicated to a child is through his or her participation in worship.

The fourth stage in Erikson's schema corresponds with elementary school age. For children between six and twelve years of age this is a time for acquiring a sense of industry as opposed to a sense of inferiority. Feelings of adequacy and self-worth and definition of one's role as girl or boy are a part of the positive developments central to this stage. In conjunction with the vast amount of cognitive learning which takes place, a child at this age will try many activities and pursue many interests. These pursuits may be short-lived, but they lead to the enhancement of a sense of industry. To be prohibited from venturing forth or to be criticized for starting things but never finishing them is to push the child toward a sense of inferiority. During this same stage the child is also venturing forth from home and parents, and entering into relationships with other adults, such as teachers and club leaders, and with peers.

This school age is a prime time for learning. The basic task of this age is to learn, to create, and to gain a sense that one will be able to contribute to life. In the context of the church's worship this is a prime time to involve children not only in learning about worship but in contributing to worship.

The fifth stage which is relevant to this discussion is adolescence, a time when the central task or crisis is that of identity formation as opposed to role diffusion. During this time of rapid and seemingly rampant physical, glandular, and sexual growth, the young person works on the question, "Who am I?" Drawing from all previous development and experience and keeping in mind one's future the teenager tries to establish his or her personality, lifestyle, values, beliefs, and commitments. With the help of peers and adult role models a sense of one's self, of identity, can be developed. Failing this, some degree of role diffusion or confusion would develop.

For a child of the covenant the church plays a significant role in identity formation. A young Christian's sense of identity is known in the context of a community with a history and purpose. Individual purpose and personality are defined in the light of God's grace, God's gifts to each person, and God's call to some form of ministry. During adolescence, when these issues are at a critical stage, the church's rituals, worship, and common life help support a young person's search for identity and affirm his or her confirmation of life in Christ.

Children Develop Mentally

The description of human development based on Erikson deals primarily with psychological and social aspects of life. Such a description needs to be matched with a description of cognitive or mental development. To know how to communicate with children in the context of worship we need to know something about how they think and how their thinking develops. For help on this task we turn to the findings of Jean Piaget.[3] Not that every perception nor every response can be measured; how a person participates in worship, or any exercise involving the mind, is never completely known, not even to the worshiper. Nevertheless, the findings of Piaget and other psychologists serve their purpose in identifying how children think and, with some degree of accuracy, how much they understand.

Piaget looks upon cognitive development as an interaction of biological givens and the rich complexities of environment and experience. A child's mind first learns to distinguish between one's self and the objects and actions around it. In the first year of life the infant is "creating objects" in the sense that the mind can think of an object and understand that the object is not a part of one's self but has its own separate existence.

As the infant grows older, more and more objects (and actions) are identified and given names. However, in the second and third years of life virtually all thinking is so specific that hardly any generalizations are made—each and every object is known individually and specifically. But the child's mind is not satisfied until some meaning and order is recognized—certain objects or actions are understood in relation to each other—Tabby and Tigger are now known not only separately but also in relation to each other as cats. And there exist in this world dogs and horses and so forth.

The attempts at understanding objects, actions, and feelings in terms of relationships is still very elementary during the years of four to seven. The child's thoughts will focus on one aspect and see a relationship because of that aspect. Sometimes the relationship, while real enough, is not all that useful. To think that Tabby and the teddy bear and the neighbor's dog are all related because each is brown in color would show that the child is growing in the ability to think, but still has a way to go in order to judge what are useful relationships and classifications.

A delightful bonus which comes with this type of thinking is that the children are capable of an imagination which is unencumbered by logic. They are free to take an image, or a daydream, or a bit of reality, and through imagination soar any distance in any direction. During these years, the naming of objects and the "creation of symbols" goes on, and as the child is exposed to more and more of life and has more experiences, names and language increase, and useful connections are made.

In the next period of cognitive development, concrete operations, as Piaget calls them, take place. Proper and useful classification of facts occur; logic is employed; and relationships, order, and organization are learned. This is a great period of learning for children, when discrete pieces of information are placed in order, according to rules. The period covers the sixth to twelfth years, corresponding in our culture to the elementary school years and to Erikson's delineation of the time for working on the issue of industry as opposed to inferiority. The ability of children of this age to learn facts and to organize these facts into meaningful wholes is immense. This is a time of the "creation of rules" to organize and explain the bits and pieces of life. A related development is an adherence to the rules—often expressed in a legalistic approach to rules and regulations. It would seem that, having learned recently what the rules are, children of this age are not about to reject them or have them treated loosely by others.

With ability to engage in concrete operations comes skill in narrative. The children are able to follow a story and to be good storytellers themselves. In earlier years a story is known and appreciated episodically, or like a series of tableaux; but now a story is relished for its development and movement toward resolution. We see this by noticing that a young child doesn't much care when she enters a movie theater or if she goes out for popcorn a dozen times. An older child wants to see a movie from the beginning, and see it in sequence through to the end.

When children become adolescents they develop their skills in abstract thinking and eventually become comfortable with what Piaget calls formal operations. They are involved in the "creation of thought." Theorizing, philosophizing, and theologizing are possible in their abstract forms. Whereas earlier such mental activities needed to be tied to very concrete situations (God loves me in the same way that Daddy and Mommy love me), during adolescence the young person can think ideally and theoretically with relative ease and without having first to "see" the situation through an actual object, event, or example. It is at this age, for example, that some of the richness of certain Christian symbols and rituals are appreciated for their subtle meanings. When Paul speaks of sin entering into our life through the old man, Adam, and of redemption coming through the new man, Christ, an adolescent just might be able to grasp the meaning and personal application of this way of explaining sin and redemption, while a younger child would be caught in and confused by a more literal way of thinking about this metaphor.

A simplified way to summarize Piaget's description of children is to show that children work at four tasks of cognitive development: the creation of objects, then the creation of symbols, then the creation of rules, and finally the creation of thought. This sequence of tasks would suggest that as much as possible activities for children need to be concrete, specific, and with reference to their own experiences. As children play or as they participate in activities (and not just talk about them or hear about them) they both learn and accomplish. When they participate in worship they will be both learning and accomplishing.

Children Participate in Worship

Knowing the descriptions of child development provided by Erik Erikson, Jean Piaget, and others enables leaders to plan worship which is appropriate and meaningful for children. This section offers some ideas about what can happen in corporate worship which includes children.

Infants are perceiving persons but do not have the power of language to communicate their ideas. They learn and think impressionistically and episodically—events are not grasped in their sequence, and the child lacks experience enough to distinguish between reality, dreams, imitations, and images. With infants and the very youngest of children, attending worship is at once a specific act and an activity with broad, not well-differentiated meanings. The child knows she is in a specific place other than home. Assuming generally satisfactory visits to the church, in time the child associates these visits with feelings of warmth, acceptance, comfort, and love.

As language skills develop, certain words and actions become more familiar and known (but not understood in an adult way). God is spoken of with reverence, or in adoration, or in wonder and awe. God is related to as Creator (and as Father, which may cause some confusion of identification). It is not possible to test what a child thinks about or knows about God. Much more may be absorbed in the person's inner self than can be expressed. A basic development is that the child begins to differentiate between something, someone, or some force referred to as God, an object with its own existence.

The child is working also on being able to have trust. The child may trust because he trusts his parents, and trusts those things, actions, and persons which the parents present to the child. Withoug knowing much of what is going on at worship, the child can still feel that it is a good place to be and a good activity worthy of trust.

Even in the first years of life the little child is gaining images and forming impressions which can serve as foundations for later learnings and attitudes. The church can strive to make the child's experiences of worship warm, accepting, rich with visual and aural imagery, and rich with routine and ritual. In later years the child will build upon these foundations.

As language skills develop, along with concomitant thinking skills, more identifications are made by the growing child. Names are given to more activities and objects. Church furnishings, being very tangible, are noted by touch and by sight and are identified. So are various activities such as hymn singing, praying, listening to the sermon, and taking part in a baptism. However, the three-, four-, or five-year-old tends to think intuitively and does not always make the correct connections. How one action follows another may be beyond her ken. This age child is notorious for the malapropisms and misplaced words she utters—words which are heard but not yet read.

These children are receptive to images. When told a story they tend to recall certain scenes and episodes, and not necessarily the whole story in sequence. Yet the images which are perceived are powerful and may, for better or for worse, influence what the child thinks of a concept or doctrine later in life. A child who has somehow gotten the image of a wrathful, punishing God, for example, will have to overcome this image in favor of a loving, accepting God. So whatever the actualities of the content of specific stories, sermons, hymns, and prayers, it is helpful to the young child to be able to worship in an accepting, comfortable atmosphere, where he is secure and can trust that the loving community worships a loving God.

Attention span is short and movement is desirable and even necessary. This child is developing motor skills and their use; it hardly is consistent to require stillness or immobility. The child of three, four, or five approaches worship as she would any activity: with curiosity, with a desire to try things out and to learn how to do things and to learn the names of things. Now that the child is able to speak in sentences, certain responses and prayers can be memorized and recited and certain hymns can be sung with confidence, particularly if they have refrains which are memorable.

If the service of worship has good pace and opportunities for physical movement, and if the minister and congregation are relaxed in the sense that some squirming and noise is tolerated, even a so-called "formal" service is an event in which young children can participate for the whole service. Perhaps the service is perceived only in episodes and there is little apprehension of the flow or time of the service, but the images, symbols, names, and associations are significant to the child. Services which are rich in tradition, including color, music, responses, and dramatic action, are more appropriate for this age than are the more austere and unwittingly sterile services of some churches.

Children of school age, ages six to twelve, move from very concrete thinking toward the ability to classify information and to discern meaningful wholes and relationships. At first the questions about worship are simple, concerning how something is done, and perhaps why. These questions are satisfied fairly well with direct replies. As the child grows there are more challenges to what adults say, and a need to see the truth for oneself. Vocabulary increases, which improves the child's ability to listen to others speaking. Reading skills also increase, as does attention span. If interest is provoked a child may spend long periods of time engaging in certain activities.

Taking all this into account, it can be said that the school-age child can participate quite well in worship—again, provided the service has the qualities of pace, movement, dramatic action, and congregational participation. The rhythm and flow of the service is known, and its rationale can be understood. For example, the reason for the placing of the recitation of the Creed at the point of congregational response is understood, as is the proclaiming of the Word through sermon, following its reading from the book. While not all words are understood and many allusions escape them, the children find the hymnbook a resource to be used, if not quite mastered. The hymnbook is itself an object of fascination (and even of salvation during lulls in the service)—there is so much information there.

Ability to think historically, in sequence and in relationships, opens up the whole matter of church history and tradition to the older child. The church year, its festivals, and the special missional characteristics of the particular church can be understood by the child and proudly accepted. Further, children at this age usually not only are willing but eager to participate in various leadership roles such as bringing forward the gifts, lighting candles, even reading aloud prayers and scripture. The child's own sense of perfection will cause him to want to practice sufficiently so as to "do it right."

As mentioned earlier, school age children are comfortable with narrative, and can both follow and tell stories. A story's structure and sequence have significance for this age child, whose cognitive development enables her to look for a beginning, a middle, and an end to the story, or a setting, a problem, and a resolution. Adults need to be warned, however, against embellishing good stories with tacked-on moralisms or sugar-coated alterations. Narratives, particularly from the Bible, have a power of their own to appeal and to stimulate. There is no need for what the noted Christian educator James W. Fowler has called the "adult blasphemy" of overtelling a Bible story.

Starting out in imitation of parents and other seasoned worshipers, the school age child gradually comes to the point of independence and self-expression. The parts of the service are taken seriously and personally: confession means a personal admission of sin; the stories of scripture call forth personal identification with the characters. The older children at this stage are not so gullible and this is one reason they will not come forward to sit on the chancel steps in those services which include a children's sermon; their sense of personal dignity is offended and their striving for perfection is threatened by being exposed in that kind of uncontrollable setting.

Children Respond to Specific Acts of Worship

Having cut across the stages of child development to see examples of how children can participate in worship, it will be helpful to consider some specific acts of worship to trace how children respond and react to these acts.

Acts of adoration, thanksgiving, and offering are usually interspersed throughout the service. This type of activity is close to the experience of children of all ages, and they can enter into such acts with basic understanding. Children have expressed "Thank you" throughout their lives and have been in awe or adoration of certain persons such as their parents from the beginning. Given basically positive experiences in worship, it would be natural for children to say "Thank you" to God in the context of worship, and to make these expressions of gratitude an offering to God. Vocabulary is of concern, in that those prayers and responses which have three- and four-syllable words will need to be learned not so much for their precise meaning but for their intent. Young children will need to be told that a certain prayer, hymn, or response is the church's way of praising God and thanking God for life, sustenance, and divine presence. (As for explaining divine presence, hardly any adults can explain that to their own satisfaction.)

Younger children will participate in acts of adoration and praise more in mood and feeling than in specific language or cognitive understanding. In some traditions it is possible and permissible for worshipers, including adults, to use more of one's whole body in expression of praise and thanks. The young child would want to smile, or to uplift arms, or to speak loudly with enthusiasm in expression of thanks. The clapping of hands, not without mention in scripture, is a customary expression of pleasure and appreciation in certain settings in our culture, but for most worship settings and worshipers this gesture does not seem right. Yet young children would find such expression direct and "natural."

The confession of sin is misunderstood not only by many children, but by many adults. Perhaps this accounts for some of the misapprehensions of the children, who learn what the adults believe about sin and its confession and pardon. It would be wrong to say naïvely that children have no sense of sin or wrongdoing, and equally wrong to say that children can understand sin in its full complexity. A look at the types of prayers of confession printed in worship bulletins would indicate that whole churches often lock in on one aspect of sin, such as that of doing wrong acts, and fail to appreciate other aspects, such as our "sinful nature prone to evil." Children at a young age already know that not all is right with them and with their relationships, even with the people whom they love the most. It should make an impression upon a five-year-old to participate with a people who dare to admit publicly their sinful condition and who respond gratefully to an assurance of pardon. The details may not be understood, but it is possible for the young child to know that while we have problems with ourselves and the way we do things, there is recourse, and we are not trapped in a condition of guilt. God is our source of forgiveness.

Older children will be able to participate verbally, reciting the prayers along with the other persons in the church. Phrases such as "miserable offenders" may at first sound foreign or even silly, but their context would suggest a significance which can be learned in due time. However, the integrity of worship is enriched if occasionally simple prayers with simple words, including prayers drafted by children themselves, are used.

With the intense desire of older children to master their world and to strive toward perfection, it is reassuring to them to have their humanity affirmed and their selves accepted by God as they are. The prayer of confession and the assurance of pardon are as deeply meaningful to children as they are to adults.

Many churches attack the problem of involving children in worship at the point of the hearing and the proclaming of the Word. The usual strategem is to provide a children's sermon. We may one day be convinced that such a practice has sufficient merit to justify its practice. For now we can see mostly problems associated with children's sermons. For one, there is the problem of overemphasis on participation at an intellectual and cognitive level, skewing the balance away from the emotive and affective levels. Especially for younger children, this is inappropriate and may leave a residue of impressions about faith as solely an intellectual pursuit. The truth is that very few children's sermons reflect much intellectual and theological integrity. Rather, they tend toward moralisms which reinforce a notion that the gospel means to be able to do the right thing in order to gain God's rewards.

A word also needs to be said in defense of the innocent, the young children who are enticed to come forward to sit with the minister on the chancel steps. In innocence they participate, answering according to their understandings the questions posed to them. Unwittingly or not, many ministers manipulate this situation and its participants; in any event, the worship of God is not easily accomplished in such practice.

Hearing the Bible read and listening to the sermon are not necessarily activities above the children's level of participation. Much of scripture is narrative, story, and parable. Even young children can listen and can derive some meaning from the reading of scripture. The weekly act of reading from scripture says to all children that the church considers the Bible to be its book. By age six or so children can know that the church seeks to order its life and mission in accordance with what is stated in the Bible. The dynamic process through which God confronts his people through their faithful reading of the Bible will not be understood in full until the adolescent years. But children will develop more and more respect for the Bible and confidence in it as they learn more about what is in it and as they participate with the congregation in its regular reading. Fifth and sixth graders are capable of clear and comprehensible reading of scripture aloud from the lectern, as a service rendered to the congregation.

Many preachers tell stories on themselves, admitting that when their children's sermons got better congregational response than did their "regular" sermons they began to simplify their "regular" preaching with good results. Well-organized sermons based on logical and obvious outlines, using a reasonable amount of simple words and personal or practical illustrations, can be understood by children, at least in part. Given a twenty-minute sermon, not many adults listen to the whole sermon or understand all of it! Some effort can be made to address the children directly, such as saying, "You who are children. . ." or "One time a six-year-old girl named Susie. . . ." As with any human encounter, personal application is likely to provoke interest. Without resorting to gimmicks, verbal, manual or otherwise, a preacher can state the gospel quite simply.

While there is no guarantee that simplicity, concreteness, vivid illustrations, and brevity will cause children to listen to a whole sermon, there is the hope that such practices will lead to more effective preaching and will not prevent children from hearing parts of the sermon. The sermon is not just for one age group, and it also should not leave out one group. "Proclaiming involves relating the word to our situation, our problems, experiencing it in the context of our lives, and this is the task of preaching. . . ." [4] In recent practice, children have not listened to sermons because sermons have not been addressed to them. Some suggestions for preparing sermons which seek to address children as well as adults are given in the final chapter of this book.

In most churches the offering is primarily a device for gathering in pledges of money. Children soon learn this to be so. Would that the offering could emphasize more the giving of self, through response, posture, and symbolism. Then children will be able to bring and to offer themselves, or some personal possession which is meaningful to them, and not just money, which may or may not have personal significance to them. At any rate, when the offering has a ritualistic aspect to it, the children find it more possible to participate. Abstractions (and commercial checks) escape them. Older children are capable of helping with worship leadership by helping collect and bring forward the gifts of the people.

Of all the acts of worship, the Eucharist or Lord's Supper is perhaps the most dramatic and hence most appropriate for children's participation. Children are drawn by the eventful character of the communion, with its tangible elements of bread and wine, all presented and shared in actively by minister and congregation. The vivid activities of the Lord's Supper are of interest and attraction even to young children. Eating and drinking are well-known experiences to be sure; sharing a meal and attributing symbolism to the meal are also experiences known to any child who has participated in a birthday party, holiday meal, or similar common social activity. Participating and belonging are associated, which is a major intention of the communion.

Younger children, with the help of their parents or other older worshipers, will sense that they are a part of the group that is celebrating the occasion. As the children get older they will learn the structure and sequence of the rite and will better be able to identify what the actions represent. *Epiclesis* and *anamnesis* may be words which escape the children's ability to pronounce and specifically to define. However, older children will understand that during communion we ask that God help us to know his presence and to recall his works on our behalf.

Some children have been known to be flippant about partaking of the elements, such as pretending that the drinking of the wine is like the way grown-ups drink, leading to drunkenness. (Adults, of course, have never been known to eat and drink flippantly—at least it has not been reported since the days of the Corinthians.) Such is the risk of any use of symbol-ism, analogy, and ritual. It can be hoped that the solemnity of the occasion and the general attitude of the congregation pro-vide an atmosphere that is respectful and serious—but not fu-nereal—which guides the partakers.

In writing about the occasion of a child's first communion, Bishop John M. Hines suggests that on the one hand, children will take communion as seriously as do the adults, and on the other hand, a service of communion (or any service) should not be so slick and polished as to allow no room for awkwardness or imperfect actions. Hines is convinced that regular participa-tion allows for growth in understanding the basic concepts of the Eucharist, those of receiving, sharing, and being thankful. The usual pattern, for worshipers of all ages, is for theology to follow and to explain experience.[5] With help from church and home, sharing and giving thanks are shown to be the inten-tions of certain acts of communion. The concept of sacrifice is harder to grasp, and may be understood after the development of abstract thinking abilities during adolescence. The Lord's Supper, for all its dramatic depiction, contains mystery beyond human ability fully to fathom; so do profundities such as the atonement. These matters will occupy a lifetime of reflection and discernment.

In a book about children and communion, Urban T. Holmes points to the very young child's ability to sense certain needs and feelings long before the skills of memory, language, and articulation are used. Not all of an infant's needs are prac-tical or physical. There are emotional and spiritual needs which are met, perhaps unconsciously, when a child partakes of communion.[6]

Without restating Holmes's long and detailed explanation of how persons perceive, and of the function of symbols in so-ciety, it can be said that the ability to reflect, make judgments, or engage in abstract thinking is not necessary for a beneficial experience of a symbol. A symbol engages us on more levels of motivation than that of reason. Holmes says that to restrict the symbol of communion to a "rational participation" is more harmful than beneficial in that it makes a univocal (single meaning) sign of a multivocal symbol.

Holmes offers several other reasons for permitting young children to take communion. There are, in his words, no "associate" or "junior members" in the one body of Christ. Children, even at age three, are particularly receptive to symbolic experiences, for there is in the children imagination and openness which allows for mystery, and even for revelation, to occur. Holmes cites Mark 10:15 as an example of Jesus' perception of the capacity of children to show faith. Anticipating a concern by some that he may seem antirationalistic, Holmes suggests that the cognitive phase during adolescence when abstract thinking is developed would necessarily be a time when a member of the church must think through critically what communion means. Not that an adolescent could ever fully analyze the symbol and the mystery, but this age would be the appropriate time for critical thought and personal decision about such meanings. And the task of reasoned search for meaning will be carried on until old age and the beginning of wisdom.[7]

4 How Children Learn to Worship

How do children learn to worship? God's presence makes worship a reality; God's gracious call initiates worship; God's Spirit enables us to respond in worship. Can we speak of learning to worship at all? Do adults have a part to play in what is ultimately God's activity in the life of a child? And if so, what is this role? How do we anticipate and cooperate with God's Spirit?

If we instruct children in the words and actions of liturgy do we run the risk of giving them only lifeless forms? Shall we as adults pursue the life of worship and let children learn by observation and imitation? Can they worship with understanding without instruction and interpretation? And if worship lacks understanding will it degenerate into mere emotion and magic?

These are important questions sending us once more to our theological foundations. Here we find the faith that calls children to worship is also the faith that leads children into worship. As the Bible issues a summons for all to bow down before God it provides models for educating children in this response.

Learning to Worship in the Hebrew Community

Specific instructions were given to the Hebrews about worship and their children's part in this life of worship. The practices were not completely consistent through several thousand years of history. Nomadic tribes, settled communities, ex-

iles, and a subject people faced widely differing situations. The
rise of the synagogue particularly brought significant changes.
The underlying principles, however, remained remarkably the
same. We will look at some of these principles in Hebrew life
and then see how they have been applied and adapted in a
Christian church today.

*The home was the center of worship; parents were the primary
instructors.* To teach children diligently that God is Lord and
that complete love is the appropriate response to him is to educate in worship. This education was to permeate their lives at
home and abroad, morning and night. The recognition of one
God and the command to love him was the lesson deliberately
taught and expressed in rituals of worship throughout the day
(Deut. 6:4–9).

Prayer was a natural part of rising, retiring, and eating.
The seasons, the harvest, and the night and day were remind-
ers of the Creator. Storytelling, conversation, and daily activities brought God's actions and commands to mind. Dress and
visual objects involved sight and touch in this process of recog-
nizing and responding.

*One day each week united the Hebrew family in worship and
learning.* The sabbath was a recurring reminder of the Creator
who rested on the seventh day. It was a sign of their special
relationship to God and an opportunity to remember, reinforced by concrete actions and abundant symbols.

Keeping the sabbath involved every member of the family.
The sabbath lamp was lit. The entire family shared a special
meal after sunset on Friday. Parents blessed their children.
Two loaves of bread were set on a clean cloth in memory of the
manna in the wilderness. No work was done. The sabbath was
an experience of worship and a way to remember why they
worshiped and whom they worshiped.

Worship was rooted in the covenant community. Parents accepted the mandate to worship and teach because they were
part of the covenant community. Though children were the responsibility of the parents, they were a trust of the wider covenant family. To be born a Hebrew was to be part of the people

created by God's gracious actions and bound in relationship to
him. Each child, regardless of sex, received the promises, the
history, and the laws which made them a special people. Puri-
fication and dedication surrounding the birth of a child were
community rituals.

The birth of a Hebrew child was an event of great rejoicing. Children were a sign of God's favor to parents and the
nation. In a patriarchal society males were naturally counted a
greater blessing. They were circumcised on the eighth day as a
sign of their relation to God and to God's people. As the years
went by other rituals came to be associated with welcoming
children. In post-biblical times one such ceremony was plant-
ing a tree—a cedar for a boy and a pine for a girl.[8]

This community celebrated its faith in religious festivals,
multimedia experiences that could never be forgotten.[9] Every
sense was involved in these occasions of worship through
drama. At Passover the family searched the house for leaven
which must be removed. The taste of bitter herbs and unleav-
ened bread recreated God's mighty acts of deliverance. During
Succoth the family built outdoor booths and relived the stories
of the wilderness days. Every branch of the lulab waved by the
child represented some part of his or her history and the provi-
dence of God. A repertoire of psalms was learned to sing praise
and to recite the community history.

Other festivals were part of Israel's life of worship: Purim,
the Day of Atonement, the Festival of Lights, and the Year of
Jubilee. Taken together they were an experience of the life of
worship—praise, penitence, encountering God in the stories of
his mighty acts, and renewed dedication.

Worship through remembrance led to obedience in the present.
Learning and participating in the community history was a
means of encountering God and an avenue for taking this worship into life. "Remember to do" is a peculiar Hebrew idiom.[10]
The Hebrews remembered they were slaves delivered by God
and from this memory flowed a kindness to strangers, widows,
and orphans (Deut. 24:17). Acknowledging God and loving
God was expressed in loving neighbor. To lead a life of wor-

ship was to lead a life of ethical conduct; to celebrate Hebrew history was to practice social concern.

Children participated in the life of worship. By the time children were three they began to memorize parts of the Torah, primarily blessings, so they could contribute to worship at home. When a boy grew large enough so that he could no longer ride on his father's shoulders from Jerusalem to the Temple Mount, he was obligated to appear in the Temple at the three required feasts.[11] Even while still a minor a Jewish boy could read the Torah and interpret it in the synagogue.

The child participated as both worshiper and learner. The activities of the home and festivals were designed to create curiosity. Actions and objects rather than words or ideas provoked the child to question. Education about worship did not precede worship, it took place in worship. To be born into a Hebrew home made a child an apprentice in worship; he or she learned by being present and taking part. Questions and answers were built into the celebration—such instruction was part of the ritual (Exod. 12:26; 13:8).

Adults and children enriched one another. Whoever teaches learns. The covenant faith required parents to explain the rituals of worship as they occurred. It was adult education in its most practical and demanding form. Ritual which must be constantly reinterpreted cannot become meaningless. As the father tells the story to the son, it is renewed in his life as well as the child's.

The requirement for worship seems to have been a questioning child and a parent who worshiped with understanding. In the experience together parent educated child and child strengthened parent. It was worship in which the God of their community history and the Lord of their daily action remained central. It was also worship in which learning was essential and relationships developed, in which children learned their identity and the conduct which expressed that identity.

The synagogue wed worship and education in public services. The rise of the synagogue, probably during the exile, created a new sphere of Hebrew learning which eventually changed the form of community worship. The emphasis changed from sacrifice to teaching. The purpose of the synagogue was teaching. The Jews gathered on the sabbath to hear the Torah read and explained. In the process, teaching became an act of worship.[12] This was to become the basic pattern for Christian worship.

By the age of four children accompanied parents to the synagogue. Nurture in the framework of worship still was centered in the home with parents adapting the Torah to the child's capacity to receive. Now instruction in the public gathering was added to this education. The sabbath became a time for community as well as family gathering. Adults and children learned together.

How did the Hebrew child learn to worship? First through a relationship with a worshiping parent, a member of a worshiping community; through intentional education built into the rituals of home and community worship; through a multitude of sensory experiences and vivid, thought-provoking symbols and dramas; through a life of ethical actions growing out of worship; through a pattern of recurring sabbath and festivals that recreated the Hebrews' story; and eventually through a form of public, community gathering which made teaching an essential part of the liturgy.

Learning to Worship in the Christian Church

The principles of nurture and worship practiced by the people of God long ago are valid today. This can be seen in the following account of a child of the new covenant living the life of worship in one particular church. As you read this account (based on actual events in several churches) look for parallels to the Hebrew experience of educating for worship.

Welcoming a Child in the Covenant Community

"I know you'll think we're silly or sentimental and you'll know I'm a very poor housekeeper," Millie Adams began the conversation as she and her daughters, Karen and Beth, sat down in Sylvia Olivera's small living room.

Millie held a bunch of brown twigs wrapped in a wet paper towel, while her slightly bewildered hostess shifted the baby to the other hip and waited to see where this conversation would lead.

"The girls and I fixed the flowers for church the Sunday Peter was baptized. I took the flowers home, put them on the mantle, and didn't look at them again for three weeks. When I was cleaning the living room last night I had to face up to those dead flowers. But, look—" and here Millie unwrapped the paper towels, "the forsythia developed roots. Somehow it seemed right that they should be the start of something growing in Peter's yard. That is, if you want them, of course."

Sylvia recalled Peter's baptism with effort. It had been a bright, cold March day. She and her husband, Rudi, had approached the occasion first of all as something that should be done. But when they talked with the minister, Dick Stevens, and read what he had given them, they caught a glimpse of what this sacrament could mean to Peter and to themselves.

"The Holy Spirit will work in Peter's life through your lives," Dick had said. "The Spirit will also work in Peter's life through the life of this church. The promises you're making are the congregation's promises too. So Peter has a much larger family now."

As the congregation stood with the Oliveras the experience had been one of new dedication, invigorating and comforting at the same time. Three weeks of colds, teeth cutting, and a husband out of town, however, had dimmed the glow.

"That's very kind of you, Mrs. Adams," Sylvia said, coming back to the present. "I . . ."

"Don't hesitate to refuse," smiled Millie. "You may feel like brown stems from a dirty living room are more like the wicked fairy's curse."

Sylvia laughed. The discomfort over stained robe and cluttered, sparsely furnished living room was fading before Karen and Beth's adoring interest in Peter and Millie Adam's self-depreciating humor.

"Oh, it's not that I don't want the forsythia. Goodness

knows, this yard is so barren it could use some plants. It's just that I don't know how long we're going to be here. Rudi's assignment to Kingsville is so temporary."

"Then that's all the more reason to plant something," interrupted Millie. "What's begun in this church with Peter will go on growing no matter where you move."

Karen spoke up with all the sophistication of a fourteen-year-old. "Mother can get a moral out of anything—a stick, a stone, or a peanut butter sandwich."

The two mothers laughed together.

"I would like to plant the forsythia. What does it take to grow?" asked Sylvia. "I'm not much good with plants."

"Sunny spot, good soil, some water during dry spells, occasional fertilizer, pruning when it gets bigger. It's a lot like raising children. Just enjoy it. It will grow in spite of you and you'll get better at looking after it."

"See what I told you," said Karen.

"The girls will watch Peter," said Millie. "I have a shovel in the car. Let's decide where you want to put his plant."

Planning for Worship in the Covenant Community

Dick Stevens tried once more to get Millie Adams on the telephone. He knew Millie's schedule as a school counselor meant errands, shopping, and visiting after 4:00 P.M. As her pastor he also knew a full afternoon and a late evening meal helped to lessen the loss and loneliness she still felt at the close of a working day since the death of her husband two years before.

This time there was an answer.

"Millie, I've been trying to get you for hours. I thought you might like to know what the worship committee has planned for your life."

"I don't think I have time for any more of your plans," Millie laughed, "but I guess it won't hurt to listen."

"There's a retreat in Oregon early this summer. The theme is 'The Life of Prayer: Personal, Public, Verbal, Silent, Active, Meditative.' "

"You sound like a brochure," said Millie.

"Well, I read one carefully because I wanted to go myself. It's a week of study and practice with the best possible leadership. We need it for our church right now. At least that's the opinion of the committee. We think you're just the person . . ."

"Oh Dick, I'd love to go, but . . ."

"Listen to all the plans before you interrupt. We have the money in the budget. Joyce and I and the Warrens are arguing over who gets Karen and Beth. The break and time away from the children will do you good. And we need the knowledge and experience you'll bring back. Think about it."

Millie had not said "yes" when she hung up, but she found herself mentally arranging transportation and clothes while she fixed supper.

Children, a Trust of the Covenant Community

Sylvia tried to decide which was harder: keeping a two-year-old in a shopping cart or keeping to a budget. She was concentrating on the price of tomatoes when she nearly collided with Joyce Stevens.

"I've been planning to come by to see you," said Joyce.

Sylvia felt the slight, irrational sense of guilt the sight of ministers or their spouses tend to arouse. It had been a month since any of the Olivera family had been in church.

"I know we haven't been to church lately. Peter's been sick and last weekend . . ."

"Stop!" Joyce held up her hand and laughed. "I haven't been keeping church attendance, and believe it or not I'm not going to ask you to do anything. I'm preschool division chairperson and I just like to keep up with our church's children. Peter's birthday—I mean his church birthday—is this month. Can you realize it's been two years since he was baptized?"

"I was thinking of that the other day," said Sylvia. "We were working in the yard when . . ." Here she interrupted herself to keep Peter from climbing out of the cart.

"This isn't the time and place," said Joyce. "May I come by Wednesday morning?"

The Life of Worship Begins at Home

"A book for you and Rudi may seem a strange birthday gift for Peter." Joyce picked up the conversation two days later almost without a break. "Right now we think helping his parents in a life of prayer is the best gift we can give Peter. Our parents group put this booklet together last year with Millie Adams' help. We know parents specialize in interrupted prayer, so you'll find this isn't the usual guide."

"We've used the book you gave us last year about how children grow in the faith. It helped us understand Peter and ourselves. It's good to know the church cares and will help us do our job. I don't know anyone who needs prayer more than the parents of a two-year-old."

Children Take Part in Advent

The fellowship hall was sanctified bedlam. Church school during the four Sundays of Advent was an intergenerational affair spilling out of classrooms into every available space. The Oliveras, the Adams, Don Harmon and his eight-year-old son Billy, Miss Mary Koehler and her mother, Mrs. Eva Koehler (celebrating her eightieth birthday that week), were making plans around the table.

"We're supposed to decorate the fourth window from the front with something that will help everyone understand what the coming of Christ means," said Rudi Olivera, scanning the task sheet attached to the table. "And we're going to be lighting the first Advent candle in the worship service today. Each group is supposed to have something to say about light. We're to read and talk about John 8:12 and Matthew 2:1–2. And I got all this backwards," confessed Rudi. "This is the first time I've led something like this."

"My mother and Karl are going to get me a bicycle and skateboard and watch for Christmas," said Billy, eager to get the group's attention.

Peter spoke up, "I'm getting a new baby for Christmas."

"Could we put a gift in our window?" asked Beth. "A big one, wrapped in shining paper?"

"Maybe the Bible verses will give us an idea of how to decorate our window," suggested Miss Mary.

"Come sit by me, Billy," invited Mrs. Koehler. "My Bible has the biggest print you've ever seen. I still have trouble seeing it. You may need to help me with some words."

Karen Adams and Don Harmon read the verses. Even four-year-old Peter had a New Testament before him with a line drawing of the Wise Men. One of the highchairs used for church suppers brought him up to the level of the group.

They talked about light and there were several objects that provided light on the table. Peter's face was aglow when he got to turn on the flashlight and when the candle was lit.

"I know one thing we could say about light," said Miss Mary, watching Peter. "Light makes our eyes sparkle."

The group finished their discussion, practiced the hymns for that morning, and set to work on their window.

"I want to light the candle and say the thing about light and put the decoration in the window," Billy stated, increasing in volume with each activity mentioned.

"We won't be here for church," reminded his father. "The service is too long for Billy," Don explained to the group.

"I don't ever have to go when I'm home with Mama and Karl," Billy said with satisfaction.

"We'll miss you both," Sylvia talked while she helped Peter model a candlestick. "Maybe you could do like Peter does. He'll leave after we light the Advent candle and go back to the nursery. You and your father could leave then too if you felt like you should."

In the pre-service fellowship and announcement time, the groups and arriving worshipers admired the windows.

"Our uncompleted window is a good symbol of all the unfinished business we have before Christmas," Millie told some people in front of their window.

As the prelude began, the sanctuary was almost dark. The

choir sang the minor lines of "O Come Emmanuel." Young people around the church lit candles in each window. The congregation responded with "Rejoice, rejoice" as the flames began to glow.

A litany was woven around the statements about light. Don and his son read together, "Our eyes sparkle and our lives shine with reflected light," and the congregation responded, "The true light is coming into the world."

Peter and Billy left after the Advent candle was lit. Both looked back as they left the sanctuary.

Children Grow in the Life of Worship

Sylvia Olivera sat down with the morning mail. Peter was in kindergarten and the baby, Maria, was asleep. She put the bills aside; no need to spoil the perfect peace of this one moment in the day. She picked up a letter from the church.

> Dear Sylvia and Rudi,
>
> Next September Peter will enter first grade. This may seem in the distant future, but you know the day is coming. Actually you've been getting ready for it a long time. His health, attitude toward learning, growing independence, and ability to work with others—all vital to his education—have been your concern since his birth.
>
> This summer you'll be doing some special things to prepare him for school: new clothes, a visit to the school, and a physical examination. Most important of all, perhaps, you'll anticipate the event with your own positive conversation.
>
> Next September is also an important date in Peter's Christian life. He will become an "official" part of the entire church family in worship every Sunday.
>
> We—you as parents and all of us as his church family—have been getting ready for this, too. Prayer, Bible reading, worship in your home, and your own

example of worshiping each Sunday have all been preparation for corporate worship.

The church has tried to support you, Peter's primary teachers. We've also tried to give Peter the love and care he has needed while at church. Part of our love has been expressed through a nursery and extended session during the morning worship.

Now he's ready for a new step. There are some definite things we can do together to help him become a full participant in corporate worship.

1. Spring quarter Peter will be studying worship in church school. He'll be in the sanctuary for parts of the service on Palm Sunday, Easter, and Pentecost. During the extended session we'll come to the sanctuary at different times and then return to our class to discuss what we have done.

2. At the end of the quarter Peter will bring home a cassette tape with responses we have been memorizing and some hymns of praise we will be using in the fall. The tape may be returned to the church when its usefulness is past. If you need a tape player, you may check one out at the church.

3. Spring quarter there will be a class for parents: "Worship for Everyone." We will think together about the theology underlying our worship, how our own life of worship can grow, and how we can help our children participate.

4. During the summer and fall you will receive the church bulletin in advance by mail. You can talk about what is going to happen in worship and reinforce what has happened in the spring quarter.

5. The first Sunday after school starts in September there will be a time of recognition for this new step in our first graders' lives. Peter will receive a hymnbook, an important tool for worship. He will then be welcomed as a full participant in the worship of our church.

6. The choir program for first and second grade begins that same week. Its primary purpose is to help children learn about music and worship. It is an opportunity to contribute leadership in the church's worship. You'll receive more information about this when the time draws near.

7. Some time during the fall Peter will be asked to assist in the morning worship: greeting people, giving out bulletins, helping with the offering, or assisting with decorations, and planning for World Communion Sunday.

We want Peter to grow in worship because we know it is essential in his Christian life. We want Peter to worship with us because we need him. Without Peter our family is incomplete and our worship is deprived of his faith and witness.

Sincerely yours,
R. J. Reno, Worship Committee Chairman
Joyce Stevens, Christian Education Committee

The Fellowship of the Worshiping Community

"You have a letter, Peter." Sylvia Olivera brought the morning mail in and Peter turned away from the television set with relief. He was still recovering from chicken pox followed by a bout of flu. He was tired of being home, being still, and being bored.

The letter was from Billy Harmon and his father. Actually, it was a church bulletin decorated with notes by Billy and a letter from Mr. Harmon. Just before the service of worship began pencils and paper were provided to write to absent or sick friends, to college students and servicemen and women, or for special celebrations like Mrs. Koehler's eighty-fourth birthday.

Peter laughed at Billy's pictures: a scowling face when he disliked the anthem, a smiling face by the sermon title, "Something to Clap About." "I clapped the loudest," was Billy's comment.

Peter studied the bulletin. They had sung a hymn he knew

and liked, "For the Beauty of the Earth." He saw the announcement that his choir would sing the next Sunday. "I'll be glad when I can get back to church," he said.

Children Lead in the Life of Worship

"I need your help reading the scripture on Sunday," Dick Stevens said to the Junior Choir. "Psalm 150 is the text for the sermon. Find it in the back of the hymnbook and we'll read it together."

The choir had been practicing a paraphrase of the psalm, "The Psalm That Swings." The children quickly noticed the difference in the Bible and the words they had been singing.

"I want to talk about praise," the minister explained. "Your song will help us 'feel' what the words mean. We want to help people think about them, too."

Together they read the psalm.

"What's a timbrel?" asked Peter.

"And a lute?" another child spoke up.

I brought pictures of some of the instruments you may not know—at least the way people think these instruments looked," Dick Stevens said. "If you don't understand a word, there's a good chance the congregation won't either. There are people much older than you who've never had the curiosity or the nerve to ask about a timbrel. Now how can we help the congregation understand the psalm?"

The choir ruled out pictures as being too small to see. They finally settled on bringing modern instruments they played: a guitar, a violin, a clarinet, and a tambourine. Beth, the high school choir assistant, offered to borrow a cymbal from the high school band. Mrs. Garcia, the director, offered to help any children who would like to express praise by dancing.

On Sunday morning the choir was ready. They had expanded the word "praise" to mean service as well as music and dance. While the choir chanted "Praise the Lord" softly there were three brief pantomimes of sharing a cup of water, welcoming a stranger, and taking clothes to the Church World

Service box. The choir repeated the last verse of the psalm and concluded with a resounding clang of the cymbal.

After the sermon they sang their anthem.

"We have a thank-you note," Mrs. Garcia told the choir the next week. "I'll read it to you and then put it on the board."

The note said:

> Dear Junior Choir,
>
> Thank you for your part in the worship service Sunday. I've never understood so clearly what praise means before. I know such leadership takes hard work. We appreciate it.
>
> > Sincerely yours,
> > Mrs. R. J. Reno

"I don't even know her," said Billy.

"You mean you don't know what she looks like," responded Mrs. Garcia. "You know a lot about her. She's a member of your church family and now she knows what praise means."

The Community Cares for the Child

Peter answered the phone. His mother was still asleep. She had been up almost every night that week with the baby. Saturday morning with Daddy out of town and Mother and Maria asleep was a little lonely. He was glad for the sound of the telephone.

"Hello, Peter." It was Miss Mary who recognized his voice. "I've missed seeing you. I know Maria's been sick the past few weeks and that you were sick before that."

"Maria's still sick and Mama's asleep," Peter said. He was slightly uncomfortable talking with an adult on the telephone. And there was something a little fearful about Miss Mary, who always sat so straight and dressed so neatly and kept all the tax records at the court house.

"Well, I really wanted to talk with you, Peter," said Miss

Mary. "Mother and I wondered if you'd sit with us in church Sunday and then have lunch with us. Billy has been sitting with us while his father is singing the Christmas music with the choir. He says he's tired of just ladies being around him."

"I'd like that," Peter answered, slightly surprised yet still pleased by the invitation. "I'll ask Mama and she'll call you."

Remembering to Do

Peter had never listened so carefully to a sermon before. Matthew 25:31–46 had been read in a different way. Peter's father had been the voice of the king in the parable; the congregation had been divided between those who had served others and those who had neglected others. They had practiced before the service, each part of the congregation having a chance to take both roles. His father's voice at the end of the scripture reading had been soft and sad.

Some of the sermon dealt with the hungry, naked strangers who were adrift in boats from Indochina. Dr. Stevens had concluded by saying their need could be the call of Christ himself to us.

During the Community Prayers that followed the sermon, Peter prayed with all his mind. He was glad Dick Stevens was saying what he wanted to say: "Dear God, please show us how to help."

The Life of Worship in Death

"I've never been to a funeral," Peter said. "I don't think I want to go. What happens?"

Mrs. Eva Koehler's death had made a lively, aggressive ten-year-old a very sober, quiet young man.

Rudi Olivera searched for the right words. He felt Peter would want to join in the service for Mrs. Koehler, yet he wanted Peter to know the choice was his.

"I guess most of our special worship services, like Maria's baptism and yours, and Karen's wedding last month, are sort of beginnings, Peter. We begin our life with God and we show that with water. We begin our life together in marriage and we show that with promises and rings. Our worship every Sunday is a beginning of a new week. Well, this worship service is for a beginning, too."

Rudi was thankful that he had read the booklet about children and death. He recalled how the parents' group had shared concerns and experiences. He remembered Millie Adams' words: "No matter how tragic the death or how deep our grief, a Christian's funeral is a joyous celebration of a quality of life we can only begin to imagine. If the service holds comfort and assurance, it should also have joy and thanksgiving. We know we have life in Christ."

"So," Rudi continued to his son, "we want to be glad for Mrs. Koehler's wonderful life with God now and remember her life with God while we loved and enjoyed her. We'll be doing the same things we've done every Sunday with Mrs. Koehler: praising God, remembering our faith, giving thanks, hearing God's word, and in a way dedicating ourselves."

Peter had felt tears and thrill when Dr. Stevens announced that Mrs. Koehler had joined the Church Triumphant. When he stood to say the Creed, his voice grew stronger. "I believe in the everlasting life."

"That's the first time I ever really said that," Peter reflected at the dinner table that night. "I'm glad I know those words."

The Community of Worship Widens

"I'll hate it," Peter said as the moving van pulled out of the driveway and the last friend had said good-bye. "I don't want to move. I don't want to leave Kingsville. I don't want to leave my school. I don't want to leave the Adams or Dr. Stevens or Miss Mary or the church. I don't care if Daddy has a promotion."

"I'll tell you a secret," Sylvia Olivera confided to her son while she gave Maria a final drink and Rudi Olivera checked the house. "I said almost that same thing when we moved to Kingsville. It was different from the city where I'd lived. The church seemed small and plain compared to my church at home. I didn't know anyone."

"How could you not like Kingsville?" wondered Peter in amazement.

"Oh, it didn't take me long to find out I had a family here. Within three months after we settled in and started worshiping in our church, I knew buildings didn't matter and we would be part of God's people here. The Sunday you were baptized . . ."

Sylvia looked up to see the forsythia bush in brilliant, golden bloom.

"We're ready," said Rudi. "Everybody in the car."

"I've got to get one more thing," exclaimed Sylvia. "Give me your pocket knife."

"We can't get anything else in the car unless you want to leave Peter or Maria behind," complained her husband.

Sylvia cut four short branches from the forsythia bush, wrapped them in a napkin from the picnic basket, and set them in Maria's abandoned water cup.

"This goes with us," she said as the car moved away from the house.

5 Leading Children into Worship Through the Home

Children learn to worship in the home.

The church is a partner with the home in this process.

As children worship at home they will also take their place in the worshiping household of God.

It's as simple as 1-2-3, *except* . . .

. . . *Except* not all children learn to worship God at home. True, they learn to worship what the adults they love and trust value, but this is not always God even when the parents are related to the church.

. . . *Except* the noun *home* needs definition. What do we mean by *home*? Is it a place where they live? Some children spend more hours in a day care center than in their own homes or apartments. Some children, due to custody arrangements in divorce, spend parts of time in two homes. Some children are really at "home" before a television set.

Home, of course, means persons, including the adults who love and care for the child physically and emotionally. But home can be one parent, two parents, two sets of parents, a relative, or a parent substitute. A nursery teacher or a babysitter may have as much influence as a parent.

With whom is the church a partner? The legal guardians or the interested grandmother who brings the child to church with her? The parents who are with the child two days a week, one of these days being Sunday, or the neighbor who cares for the child from daylight to dark five days a week? The parental relationship in actuality may be divided among several adults who are related to one another only through the child.

. . . *Except* there can be no partnership with only one partner. We are fully aware that the church often fails in its responsibility to support the home in the task of leading children into worship. But many homes are indifferent or unwilling partners. Any church school roll represents a wide spectrum of commitment, from parents who are vitally related to Christ and his church and covet this relationship for their children to parents whose primary interest is in having reasonably safe, free babysitting while they read the Sunday newspaper in peace.

. . . *Except* not all home worship is related to congregational worship in the understanding and practice of parents. Many Christian adults consider their worship a private affair. A deep streak of individualism separates their prayers to God from the prayers of the community of God. They want their children to seek God in prayer, to hear God speak, to give themselves to God, but for them this has no connection with corporate worship.

Arlo Duba, Director of the Chapel at Princeton Seminary, describes the phenomenon of "Seminarians Who Have Never Been to Church." [13] The church boom of twenty-five years ago required duplicate services of worship. Church school and worship occurred simultaneously. Though the need has ended the pattern has continued. Education is chosen for the young and worship for the more mature.

Says Duba, "There are many young people who get to or perhaps through high school without ever having had an opportunity to worship, to become acquainted with hymns, to hear the Bible preached, to sense their oneness with an intergenerational body of believers. Their church experience is homogeneous, graded first as pre-school, then primary, then junior." [14]

The link between home worship and the gathered church is not always understood. For many church members the individual and the home are entirely separate from the body of Christ in acts of devotion and praise. These exceptions must be kept before us as we plan ways to work with the home in leading children into worship.

Principles for the Home-Church Partnership in Worship

We believe we are called to worship as families and as the church family. We want our children to worship with us. We want to work through the primary channel God has provided for worship education: the home. How shall we do this? What principles support sound practices? What strategies shall we employ to invite, support, and educate the home?

Our first principle is this: Children learn in the home. This has been evident since the first mention in the Bible of religious education in Hebrew homes. Walking, talking, and working in the rhythm of the day's activities and in the silent symbols around them, children will grow in worship. Most children will hear God's call to worship at an early age through the adults they love and trust. When parents recognize and respond to God, young children imitate, then join in the acts and attitudes we call worship.

It happens in the quietest and subtlest of ways. Day by day the ones who are close to the child look beyond themselves to One who is close to them. A hymn sung while dishes are washed, a record played, a book read, a creche lovingly unpacked at Christmas, or a gift offered to someone in need are unspoken testimony to the adults' trust. The unseen One is thanked at meals, consulted in decisions, sought in crisis, and included in joy.

Gradually a pattern takes shape: there are special times to be with God at home; a special time and place to be with others who trust God too; special seasons to rejoice in what the One who is always present has done. Gradually, too, a Person emerges, opening his arms to children, feeding the hungry, enjoying birds and flowers, healing the sick, and stilling the storm.

With little formal or planned instruction the young child is drawn into worship just as he or she is drawn into speech. Before they can read or write, children can have entered the profoundest experiences of worship—joy, confession, forgiveness, acceptance, and dedication.

The pattern of living, loving, and leading must always be before the church. When a child's home does not offer this, any substitute we try to offer must be built on this principle of a child related to a worshiping adult.

A second principle is this: We must adapt our ministry of support to the variety of homes we serve. We cannot and should not usurp the role of the home in a child's life, even when we invite the child to an experience the home rejects. It is a temptation to criticize adults who show no concern for worship or to judge those whose lifestyles are built on values we question. Our task is not to remake homes to fit one pattern, particularly a pattern that fits our opinions and plans. We must look for evidences of God's work in every home and build on and cultivate the strength there.

Our plans must be as diverse as our children's homes.

An affluent family is on vacation three months each year on a secluded island resort; a church school teacher mails them a church bulletin each week with a few comments penciled on the margin.

A mother's work schedule requires one Sunday a month on the job; another family picks up her children on those Sundays and returns them home after lunch eager to tell their mother what happened at church.

A mother and father feel uncomfortable about their children's behavior in church; an intergenerational retreat with worship in an informal setting and opportunities to know older members lessens their concern.

A new family in town is unhappy in a new and different church setting; the pastor visits, goes over the order of worship, and explains "why we do things this way and how we adapt this basic plan to different situations."

A father has grown up in a different tradition of worship; a class on worship allows him to explore and evaluate his church's own tradition.

A serious illness occurs; the family receives a card of love and concern and a statement, "We prayed for you in the Prayers of the People on Sunday."

The paths into worshiping in homes are as numerous and varied as the homes. Some are carefully planned educational ventures and some are informal encounters. Some are thoughtful friendship. Some are ministry in crisis. The whole church is involved, from pastor to every member who worships.

As we plan specific approaches and programs to educate and support families in worship we will keep in mind the home, the center where God first calls children to worship, and the varied homes God calls to worship in our particular congregation.

Strategies for Working with the Home

Our first strategy can be to nurture the adults who nurture the children. Worshiping adults lead children into worship. This suggests vital congregational worship, inviting parents into God's presence. Parents need opportunities to study about prayer, theology, Bible, and worship. They need opportunities to serve as liturgists and choir members. This may mean a nursery during rehearsals and planning sessions or a friend to sit with their children on these occasions. There should be a welcome for children of all ages and care for these children when it is appropriate.

The emphasis here is not on parents as teachers of children; it is on parents as children of God with needs to praise, confess, hear, and dedicate themselves in a fellowship of believers. Pastoral and educational leadership will help them apply the liturgy to their daily lives.

Our second strategy can be guidance in home worship. Expertise in worship education does not automatically follow the birth of a child. Parents who worship regularly may have difficulty expressing what they know about worship. They may expect too much of children, or too little. They may secretly believe the hasty "thank you" to beat the first bite of a meal is valued less by God than the formal prayer of the sanctuary. A three-minute attention span may seem too brief to make a Bible story worthwhile.

The church can help parents develop realistic expectations and resources to meet different ages and abilities. A church library can offer books, records, tapes, games, and pictures. We can help families in establishing rituals and celebrating holidays so these times become both a recognition of and response to what God is doing.

We may need to eliminate some meetings or ask parents to do less so they will have time to cultivate the life of worship at home. There is merit in the Mormon idea of one family night a week with no television, outside recreation, or meetings, including church meetings.

In one church an intergenerational study of prayer provided a valuable resource for home worship. All ages listed important events in their lives. The events included a new baby, the first day of school, learning to ride a bicycle, a new house, entering high school, the beginning of a vacation, a new job, a serious illness, the death of a pet or a loved one, and getting married. The group divided the list of events and in teams of two or three persons they wrote prayers for each event. Another evening they listed all the persons who had helped them or touched their lives that day: teachers, doctors, bus drivers, truck drivers, telephone repair crew, relatives, and others. Again prayers were written, expressing thanks and petition.

Out of this study a book of prayers for all ages was printed. It was drawn from the community life and was relevant to the situations all homes faced each day.

"Family worship would never work at my house," said the father of three boys. "We don't sit still long enough." A few weeks after this remark was made in a class on worship, the family was invited to a fellow class member's home. As the two families came to the table the host said, "We usually join hands and tell the thing we've liked best about the day." It was an easy and comfortable sharing of good test grades, a long distance call, a pretty sunset, and other events and accomplishments. From four through forty, each person contributed. The host concluded with the words, "And God, we thank you for this food, too." It was genuine worship and a demonstration as well. Family worship could take place without formality and absolute control by parents.

A third strategy can be a clearly stated policy or intent about children and congregational worship. We are diligent in enrolling our baptized children in nurseries and church school classes. Every child receives a card about the choir program or summer camp or vacation church school. Why are we so indefinite about inviting children to congregational worship?

The church cannot and should not dictate what parents do with their children. But without some statement about how and when children can begin to worship with us, most parents will assume that the deciding factor is when their children will not bother anyone. Or they may conclude that they should wait until children achieve a certain level of understanding, with some vague notion of a readiness test. Some assume we wait until children ask to come. Many parents leave their children in nurseries and kindergarten and even in upper elementary grade child care programs rather than bringing them to corporate worship. When a church has no plans or directions, it would seem pleasant for the child and easy for the adults not to bring the child.

When the church pursues the course of offering worship and church school at the same hour, then we have a very questionable policy. Quoting Arlo Duba again, "In actual practice this promotes an assumption which I hope none of us would endorse. It says that the Christian, young or old, needs only one or the other, worship *or* Christian education." Our practice produces Christians "who do not see worship as important to the Christian life," and encourages "the mentality that wants to fulfill all religious obligations in one hour." [15]

Too frequently bad policy or no policy has been our way. We need, as a church family, to think positively and definitely about when and how children can best enter congregational worship. Are babies welcome in the sanctuary? Is alternate care provided for them? If so, why? And if it is provided must it be used? Can a three-year-old benefit from the processional hymn or a joyful anthem by a junior choir? Can this be noted in advance in the church newsletter or bulletin? Are parents comfortable taking a child from the service after ten minutes? Can the congregation be helped to understand this as a purposeful activity and not as disinterest or insensitivity to the spirit of worship? Are festive occasions a good introduction for kindergarten children? Can a note be sent, helping parents prepare a child for these occasions, noting certain things to observe and talk about? Do we want elementary children to worship regularly? Can we state this and provide recognition for the occasion?

In small congregations with few children, the minister may simply counsel with the parents, but he or she needs the thoughtful decisions of the session or worship committee behind the counsel. Larger churches with larger numbers of families and children may need to undertake more comprehensive publicity and education.

These policies are not laws arbitrarily dictated. They represent the same concern as shown in good planning for church school or other activities. They help parents know what is possible, what is reasonable, and what is helpful. Such prayerfully developed plans make it clear that we love our children and want them to worship God. This expression of the entire church's hopes and expectations interpreted to parents may be one of our strongest strategies of support.

Finally, and partly as an outgrowth of our third strategy, *we can support families in worship with planned education about worship.* Such education can take place in many settings: church school, church night suppers, church retreats, neighborhood clusters, and intergenerational studies built around the church year.

Here two plans are sketched briefly with a look at some learning activities in each.

A Course for Parents: Worship with Our Children

"Worship with Our Children" was a course designed for parents of rising first graders, although any interested parent of kindergarten or elementary children was invited to attend. The study, a church school elective, was scheduled for the six Sunday mornings following Easter.

Parents received a letter explaining the church's hopes and plans for children to grow in worship. It included a definite date in the fall to celebrate the first grade child's regular participation in worship with us. "Let's plan for this together," the letter invited.

Session I. Worship: What Does the Bible Say?

The opening session was based on a study of verses in Deuteronomy, Psalm 100, Isaiah 6:1–8, and Acts. The study emphasized the centrality of worship in the formation of Israel as a people and the meaning behind the forms this worship took. The class saw the development of the synagogue, and the early church at worship in Acts.

Session II. Worship: What Does the Church Say?

A sketch of the development of worship in church history was presented; then the class looked at the Reformation and the Reformed understanding of worship, our denominational directives for worship, and our own church's procedures for planning worship.

Session III. Worship: What Do I Say?

In this session parents examined their own attitudes about worship in a nonthreatening way to see what worship could mean to them. With church bulletins before them, the participants were asked to translate each event in the order of worship into a sentence which would contain God as subject or object, or the first person plural pronoun as subject or object, and a verb. Some examples: "Prelude—We prepare to worship God." "Assurance of Pardon—God forgives our sins." "Creed—We pledge allegiance to God." Each statement was printed on a separate card.

The next step was to arrange these cards in the order of importance for the participant personally. Each person was asked, "Which part of the service has the most meaning for you? Why?" The parents examined the various values expressed in these orders, then planned an order of worship based on what had meaning for the group. The outcome underscored the soundness of the church's basic plan for worship.

Session IV. Worship: What Do Children Say?

The walls were decorated with pictures children had drawn of worship services they had attended and statements they had made about worship. These were the background for a presentation on the needs and abilities of children at different stages of development. With this information as background, the class discussed how congregational worship might be perceived by a child and what it could mean to him or her.

Sessions V and VI. Worship: How Can We Prepare?

The last two classes provided practical suggestions for helping our children worship with us. A poster displayed a magazine advertisement for an encyclopedia. The picture showed an expectant mother and father surrounded by a baby bed and the clothes, equipment, and supplies necessary for a new baby. The parents were reading and the caption said, "It's never too early to start preparing your child for school."

The parents made a list of how they had or would prepare their children for the first day of school. It included such things as:

> *Long-Range Preparation*
> Good health care, opportunities for development in self-confidence, group relationships.
> Reading, picture books, Mother Goose rhymes.
> A target date, knowing school is required and when.
>
> *One-Year Preparation*
> Enrollment in a good nursery school.
> Sesame Street, educational television.
> Positive comments about learning and school.

Handling paper, pencil, scissors.

Opportunities to make things, develop skills.

Learning the alphabet, printing one's name, calling attention to letters.

Immediate Preparation

Physical examination.

Visit school.

Meet teacher.

Make sure they know at least one child in their class.

Positive comments and anticipation. Talking about what will happen.

Buying school clothes for comfort.

Buying supplies.

Lunch money and lunch.

Good night of sleep, regular bed time.

From this list it was obvious that parents had a commitment to education. They understood its necessity in a child's life and positively built toward its success.

The group was then asked to list what steps we take to prepare our children for congregational worship. We know a vital aspect of the Christian life is corporate worship; we know children must begin to worship with the congregation at some point; the church has set first grade as the target date. How do we prepare our children?

The contrast in the two lists was apparent. The group began to build a list by paralleling some of the preparations we make for school.

The last session concluded with these words: "For the next several years you will be worshiping through your ministry to your own child. As you answer questions, guide young eyes across a page, locate a scripture, or point out a place in the bulletin, do not mistakenly feel you have interrupted your worship, or feel you are interrupting the worship of others. Remember, the One whom we worship said, 'Whoever welcomes in my name one such child as this, welcomes me.' "

A Class for Parents and Children: We Worship God

During September and October first and second graders and their parents studied congregational worship together. In the church school hour grown-ups and children selected learning activities planned to help them explore concepts of worship and learn about worship in their own church.

Learning centers and activities were built around six main ideas: praise—the reason we worship; the church family in which we worship; persons who lead us in worship; our special time and place for worship; acts of worship; and the sacraments. The first session focused on the concept of praise. For the second session all centers were built around the idea of the church as a family of praisers. On the following Sundays, selection of centers could be made in any order.

Session I. Praise God

Praise is the attitude that lies at the heart of worship. God has loved and redeemed us; we respond in love, joy, and gratitude. This was the starting point for our family study of worship. The centers were designed to help students focus on God, our reason for praise, or on ways we can praise.

1. *We See God's Love When* . . . . Participants contributed to a large wall mural of evidences of God's love through drawings or selecting from an assortment of pictures including scenes of families, material gifts, nature, Jesus, and the church.

2. *A Song of Praise.* Families made a rebus of the Doxology and covered it with plastic to use at the family table for mealtime blessings.

3. *Words of Praise.* Alleluia, Amen, Rejoice, Love, and other key words were cut from tagboard and mounted. Participants made rubbings of these words (a form of printing familiar to anyone who ever placed a coin under a paper and rubbed over it with a pencil). The words were matched with words on a bulletin board. These words gave clues for finding the word in Bible, hymnbook, tape, or record. A by-product of this

vocabulary-building exercise was the demonstration to parents of young children's ability to recognize words in certain contexts although they were not part of their reading vocabulary. Families could decorate pieces cut from a magnet strip to mount their praise words on the refrigerator at home.

4. *Ways to Praise.* On a bulletin board were placed pictures of sports events, a child trying on a dress her mother had made, a husband giving a gift to his wife, etc. On a tape recording were responses that could be made to these pictures: the cheers of a crowd as a touchdown is made; clapping; a verbal thank-you; a statement, "I love you." Students matched the responses and pictures.

5. *Practicing Praise.* This activity was designed to give meaning to the word *praise* by beginning with experiences familiar to almost any family. The center included a leader, four to six chairs in a circle, a three-minute timer, and score sheets mounted on the wall. The object of the game was to say as many good things about members of the group as possible in the designated time. The wall was decorated with a number of incomplete sentences in bright colors, such as:

> What I like most about you is . . .
> I'm happy to be with you because . . .
> I think you're great because . . .
> One thing you've done that I like is . . .
> You made me happy when . . .

The leader and scorekeeper introduced the game by saying: "Praise means saying something good to someone or saying something good about someone. Most of us praise every day. We already know how. But like any good thing we do, praise needs practice." The leader explained the object of the game and kept score. The family with the highest praise score at the end of the hour received blue ribbons with "PRAISE" lettered on them.

When the time was up (usually there were two three-minute periods, with improved performance in the second period) the leader helped the group reflect on what they had done: "Sometimes it's hard to think of good things about a person even though we know many good things. It's hard to select just one. When you're praising someone you think about them and not yourself. You have to know something about the person to praise them honestly. Praise that you don't really mean doesn't count, but sometimes when you say something you find you mean it. You feel good when you praise someone else."

The leader concluded, "When we worship we praise God. No one keeps score. When we're all together we remember what God has done. We think about how God loves us. We look at the beautiful world God has given us. Then we use words, songs, smiles, gifts, and thoughts to say: 'We love you. We like the things you do. We're happy to be with you. We think you're great because. . . .' "

A Sanctuary Tour

Included in the learning activities was a sanctuary tour to help the students recognize the sanctuary as a special place with a special purpose. The students were helped to become acquainted with the furnishings and symbols, to learn what these things told about worship, and to feel at home in the sanctuary.

Among the worship furnishings and objects considered by the group were the choir loft, pulpit, pulpit Bible, paraments, hymnbooks, symbols, pews, communion table, baptismal font, narthex, contents of the pew racks, and organ. Several small suitcases with appropriate travel labels were prepared. A family chose one of these and went to visit the empty sanctuary. The suitcase contained a master card or "ticket" to be marked as each object was found or activity completed, an instruction sheet, and cards with a word or a picture of worship furnishings to be found.

For one activity a small pencil was taped to a card with these instructions: "Find one of these in the sanctuary. How would you use this in worship? Tell your group."

A picture of the baptismal font had these instructions: "Find this in the sanctuary. Stand beside it. Tell everyone when you would use it in a service of worship."

A picture of a pew had these instructions: "What is this called? Choose the place you like to sit. Invite everyone to come sit there with you."

A catalog of church furnishings and supplies was a good source for pictures. With the pictures, young children could receive assignments without having to be able to read. The sanctuary tour as well as the entire study was enriched by large photographs of the sanctuary and of the congregation at worship taken and printed by a young member of the church. Several instruction cards in each suitcase included such photographs.

A special note: Several first and second grade church school pupils had parents who could not or chose not to take part. Other adults were found who took part in the learning activities with these children and then invited the children to worship with them in the hour that followed.

6 Teaching About Worship in Graded Groups

We want our children to worship with us. How can we help them participate with understanding? Structured learning in classes graded by age is an important means of teaching in the church. Can learning in age groups be used to lead children into meaningful worship? The answer to this is a positive "yes" as long as we remember two things:

> —The response of Christian worship is always the work of God. We do not create or control this response.
> —Instruction is never a substitute for joining with those who worship. Worshiping with others is the indispensable means of nurture.

This means joining with the total church on special occasions for the preschool child and joining regularly in corporate worship for the elementary school child. It is in the midst of the church at worship that a child will observe and be stimulated to ask, to imitate those he or she loves and trusts, and to catch the spirit of the gathered household of God. A classroom cannot create this situation.

What Graded Education Can Do

Graded education can be an efficient and effective way of helping children take part in worship. When we group children by age we can tailor our objectives and methods to their abilities and needs. We can consider their style of learning and accommodate our teaching to this.

Some important contributions such structured learning can make to enabling children to worship are:

1. *Building a vocabulary of worship.* The church needs to decrease the number of obscure, abstract words used in the liturgy. At the same time, children need to increase their vocabulary so they can respond to God through varied words and ways. Expanding vocabulary is a major task through kindergarten and elementary years. We need make no apology for teaching children "hard" words and how to use them. *Holy, alleluia, praise, doxology, confess,* and *dedicate* are only a few of the words children can come to use with understanding and satisfaction.

2. *Acquiring skills.* We assume children need to be taught how to read, how to use an index, and how to punctuate a sentence. Many skills we use in worship can be taught just as we teach subjects in school. It is reasonable to plan a school study unit on how to use a dictionary. It is equally reasonable to plan a unit on how to use a hymnbook. A few of the skills we can teach children are how to voice a prayer, how to listen, how to anticipate a sermon, how to use silence, how to use a bulletin, and how to find a scripture verse in the Bible.

3. *Memorizing and using responses.* Some parts of our worship are repeated frequently and are almost universal. The Doxology, the Gloria, the Lord's Prayer, and the Apostles' Creed fit this category. Children can memorize and use these responses apart from the actual worship service so they know the words and the source of the words.

4. *Anticipating events in worship.* Talking about and "walking through" a worship service, an ordination service, a baptism, or Worldwide Communion will create a readiness for the experience. Children will look for specific things. They will be comfortable because they know how to act and what to do.

5. *Interpreting what has been seen and done.* Children who have taken part in worship benefit from sharing questions and ideas with other children like themselves. To a classroom situa-

tion they will bring the motivation for finding why the Bible is central in our worship or why the color of the paraments in the sanctuary is green. Working together is a stimulus. Confession and pardon have very specific meanings for a six-year-old. These can be comfortably explored with like minds.

6. *Making plans to contribute to worship.* A group of children can write a prayer. A class can decorate a window or communion table. Together children can plan for singing, speaking, praying, or giving in a way a single child will seldom do. One class knew the sermon text in advance and planned an illustrated bulletin for that Sunday. Their contribution as a class enriched the understanding of the total congregation and gave the children a stake in the sermon that guaranteed active listening.

Planning for Graded Worship Education

Once we understand the limitations and possibilities in age-group learning about worship, we can begin to select schedules, content, and methods. Several principles can be kept in mind.

1. *Know the children.* The information about children in chapter 3 is part of the background you will need. Studies of child development will help us know what is needed and apt. We must be sure to add our personal observations as well. We will be leading children in particular, not children in general. If you plan to think of the church as a family, know the home and personal situations of the children you teach. If a child has a severe reading problem, find a way to present vocabulary in some way other than the written word.

2. *Know and work with existing curriculum.* Most church school materials have worship study units and concepts built in. Kindergarten and early elementary studies deal with praise and thanksgiving. There will be studies on prayer, the history of the church and its worship, the Bible as God's Word, and repentance and forgiveness in elementary grades. Worship education is not a separate track from the other edu-

cational work of the church and must be planned in conjunction with it. Some units of study can be reinforced and
related to worship as they are taught in the church school;
some units can be set for special study; and some units can be
combined to make a comprehensive course for other situations such as family camps or Wednesday night intergenerational studies.

3. *Use the life of your church as curriculum.* A baptism is
scheduled. This is the time to teach about baptism. The church
mobilizes leadership and information for an emphasis on stewardship. This is the time to teach about the response of dedication. A wedding, a funeral, an ordination service, or the
dedication of a building are all occasions that can be used to
enrich our understanding of responding to God.

4. *Adapt all curriculum for your local church.* Shaping materials to fit the situation is such a common principle of good
teaching that it is probably unnecessary to mention this. The
purpose of this education, however, has very specific application. We want children to worship in the church family where
they are. If first grade children study an order of worship, it
should be the order of worship they actually will follow. A
hymn study guide is of little value if it does not help the child
with the hymnbook he or she will use. Hence, any resources
you draw from must be carefully adapted to your church. Pictures of your congregation at worship will be more helpful than
pictures from magazines or church publications. Tapes of your
choir in song will achieve your goals more effectively than a
recording of a massive choir singing responses you will never
use.

A Model for Teaching Kindergarten Children About Baptism

Much of the theology surrounding baptism is beyond the
grasp of children from four to six years of age. They may hear
of the washing away of sins or the death and resurrection of
the believer with Christ, but they cannot apply this and probably will literalize it. On the other hand, the idea of initiation

into the household of God or of belonging is well suited to their understanding and experience.

Many children of this age have younger brothers or sisters. Some may remember their siblings' baptisms. They know the joy, responsibility, and difficulties a new baby brings. They have stepped into groups outside the family and can reflect on what being a member of a family means. Their world is growing wider each day and they need the security of knowing they, too, are a part of the household that loves and cares for little ones no matter what they do or how much trouble they are. And, like all children of this age, they love to measure how much they have grown and how much they can do in contrast to their babyhood.

The Situation

The kindergarten teachers knew a month in advance of the Gordon baby's scheduled baptism. The weather was warm and colds and germs were at a minimum. The advance notice allowed them to conclude the present unit of study and to notify the parents of the special emphasis and schedule.

One of their pupils came from a single parent home and one child lived with grandparents. The teachers were sensitive to making the term "family" fit many situations. Three children had not been baptized and teachers needed to make sure nothing was said that would make them feel inferior.

The Schedule

The five hours for this study took place on two Sunday mornings during the regular church school hour and the extended session coinciding with congregational worship. The activities were planned to fit the usual routine with large blocks of time for play and learning center choices, some time for talking and planning together as a group, and ample time for physical needs—rest, snack, cleanup, and toilet.

Room Arrangement

The room had block and home living centers which remained unchanged. Both centers had pictures of families or adults and children at work and play together. The block center had dowels of different widths and lengths to represent people in families. The home living center added a baby doll and crib.

There was also a "Look and Listen" center with the book, *A Very Special Day*, a book about Jesus and the children, and a filmclip entitled *Baptism and Communion*.[16] The center included a typewriter and a teacher so children could dictate ideas, questions, or observations. Other centers were provided as needed.

Main Ideas
1. The church is the household of God.
2. The church is a family of many families.
3. Baptism is a sign we belong in God's family.
4. Jesus told us to use this sign.
5. We use water to baptize babies and grown people. Water reminds us of good things.
6. Baptism tells us God loves this very baby.
7. We have a part in baptism.

The First Sunday
Main Ideas 1 to 4 were the focuses for the first Sunday.

In one corner of the room a large box stood with just enough painted detail to distinguish it as our church. Two tables near the box were ready for the children. On one there were pieces of paper (approximating the shape of bricks) and crayons. Children drew pictures of their families and began to paste the bricks on the church.

On the other table were pictures of church members cut from a pictorial directory. The pictures included the minister and individuals and families known to the children, but also several persons not known. One was a picture of a shut-in. The children selected and pasted pictures of these people on bricks so they could be seen as part of the church.

In the "Look and Listen" center the words "House of God" had been put above a picture of our church; the words "Household of God" had been put above a picture taken during a church picnic.

When the group gathered to the music of "For the Beauty of the Earth" the leader showed these two pictures. Referring to her Bible she said, "These words have been used to describe the church for a long, long time. A man named Paul wrote a letter to the church long ago. He said even though you are all different and have different things to do, you all have been called to be a part of the household of God. Even though you are part of the Rios household or the Jones household or the Koutsous household, we all belong together in one big household that is God's.

We walked around the box church discussing our pictures and the friends we had selected. Did we all look alike? Were we the same age? What different things did we do? Did we have to know a person for them to be part of the household of God? We held hands around the church and sang the first, second, and last stanzas of "We Are the Church" by Avery and Marsh.

During snack time we discussed plans for seeing our church family, or the household of God, together. The children had been in the sanctuary during the morning worship and were familiar with the gathered church. We planned to look for specific things so we could talk about the church when we returned. We were to look for someone we knew; for someone we didn't know; for someone older; for someone young; and for something everyone did together. We were also to say "hello" to anyone near us as we took our seats.

We had reserved the front row of the balcony so children could have a good view. We remained through the opening hymn of praise.

During the second hour children moved about the learning centers. They could dictate a sentence to the teacher at the typewriter about the church. Some children chose to draw pictures of all the families together. As the second hour drew to a close the group shared pictures and sentences about the church.

Then we thought about "How do you know you belong to

the church?" A typical answer was "You just do," or "Your mother tells you." We talked about ways of showing you were really Jane who belongs to the Davis family. We had a birth certificate which is taken to school. They examined a wedding ring with initials on the inside to show a married couple belong together. We had a church stamp and we stamped the church's name on each child's hand in watercolor ink.

Then, using the picture of Jesus and the children in the book from the "Look and Listen" center, we said Jesus had told us the way to show we belong to his household. He had come to say God loves us and wants us all to be in his household. Baptism is the special sign he told us to use. Some children had seen the filmclip about baptism. (It was set up to be seen as an individual child turned it. The script was not used.)

Children contributed what they knew about baptism. We then anticipated next week's baptism with them and said that God gave the church a part in each baptism. We closed with the second stanza of "For the Beauty of the Earth."

The Second Sunday

The routine of the second Sunday varied. The children who chose to do so played outside. A small pan of water had been added to the home living center so dolls could be washed, and a low screen of pictures showing water had been placed by the rug where the children would gather. The pictures showed swimming, boating, a lake, rainfall, birds in a birdbath, and a waterfall.

After about twenty minutes we called the children together. A teacher stood by the door with a pan of water and a towel so children could clean their hands. We gave each child a small cup of water from a pitcher of ice water.

Then we talked about water and eventually put our statements into a song, sung to the tune of "For the Beauty of the Earth" (Dix) and using the refrain as written. We talked about why water was a good "sign" for showing we belong.

The minister stopped by briefly to ask the children to help him welcome a new baby into our church family. He had the baptismal bowl and explained what he would do and what he would like for them to do.

The Gordons had been invited to stop by with Holly before going into the sanctuary. We prepared our snack, setting a place for the Gordons and talking about what we could do to make Holly comfortable. (No loud noise. Ask if you can touch her and be very soft. Would the sunlight be too bright?)

The visit was a happy experience. Holly responded to the young faces. She lay on a pad on the rug while the children sat around her and the Gordons talked about what the sacrament of baptism meant to them and to Holly. They explained that as Holly's big brothers and sisters the children could help her.

The children sat on the front row in the sanctuary. The minister asked them to come forward and represent the household of God. He repeated Holly's full name and talked about its importance. "No one else is like Holly Anne Gordon. God made each child special." Then the children said "welcome" to Holly using her full name.

After the baptism we drew pictures about the sacrament and combined our statements about the church, water, and baptism into a book. The statements were typed by a teacher. Pictures were drawn by children and traced by a teacher on the stencils so the book could be mimeographed.

We decided to give a book to Holly and her family so they could remember this special day. During the week the teachers combined the pages into a book. The children colored their pictures for the gift booklet and then we covered these pages with clear plastic. This was completed the following Sunday during the opening moments. Any pupils who were absent received the books by mail.

A satisfactory postscript: The Gordons sent the class a thank-you note and a picture of Holly that was added to the box church in the corner. The baptism booklet was placed on a shelf in the library so children and adults could learn about baptism. The children received a thank-you from the librarian and stopped by to see their book with pride.

Studying the Order of Worship in Elementary Grades

Ask a first grader why we go into the sanctuary and the answer will be something like this: "We come here to sing," or, "We come here to pray."

Ask a sixth grader the same question and the reply probably will be, "We come here to worship God."

The second answer is more satisfactory theologically, but the first answer is exactly right for the six-year-old.

During the span of time we call the elementary school years children are accumulating a multitude of facts and skills. It is prime time for learning. But a first grader, a fourth grader, and a sixth grader each will use these facts differently. (Refer back to chapter 3.) The way of thinking changes. Even when we teach about the same subject, we approach it differently.

The following study and activities are all based on the order of worship we find in our church bulletins.

Church bulletins usually are adult reading material. Spacing and print size are seldom planned from a young reader's viewpoint. Vocabulary presents a problem at the beginning, but this can be overcome. The major difficulty with bulletins is that they describe worship abstractly as a series of occurrences outside the worshiper, rather than concretely as a group of actions in which we all take part. Worship is presented in a way that encourages observation rather than participation.

In helping children to follow and understand the order of worship it is important to keep worship before them as a verb rather than a noun. If bulletins can be modified to accommodate children, this simplifies the learning process (and usually benefits the whole congregation as well).

A Design for Introducing First Graders to the Order of Worship

With few exceptions first graders are ready to join in the liturgy of the church. They will approach the experience as first graders, seeing separate actions rather than the cluster of responses to God we call worship. We may yearn for them to glimpse the transcendent God. They will settle for the sight of a friend. We want them to give their lives to God; they concentrate with frightening intensity on getting a nickel in the offering plate.

These active six-year-olds are busy learning words, seeing one thing at a time, and wanting to know what to do without seeking the reason behind the act. This way of thinking is God's plan for their growth. Enjoy it. Use it. Cultivate it. Praise it.

First graders can count, follow directions, "read" pictures in sequence, and read a few written words. Moreover, these first graders desperately want to be "in" as knowledgeable members of the group. They want to take part like a "pro," not a beginner. When they know how, they love to participate.

These considerations helped to shape the following study.

The Situation

The session described here is part of a series of thirteen sessions designed to prepare first graders for worship. At the conclusion of the sessions they were recognized and welcomed as regular worshipers in the congregation with specific contributions to make and leadership roles to assume.

The Schedule

Eight of these sessions took place during the church school hour, five took place as extended sessions at church night suppers. The entire course was completed in two months. This session came on the third Sunday morning. We had slightly more than an hour for this as the children stayed through the twenty minutes between church school and the worship service.

We always served refreshments, did something very active, then gave them their worksheets and let them join their parents or sit with a teacher in the sanctuary. Parents knew about the worksheets and how to help the children with them.

Main Ideas
1. We can make plans and follow them together.
2. When the people of the church gather they have a plan for worship.
3. This plan helps us act together.
4. This plan tells us to sing to God, pray to God, hear God's Word, and give to God.
5. We can follow this plan and join in the worship of God.
6. The church bulletin gives us this plan each Sunday.
7. The Bible helps us make our plan.

The Session

As children arrived they could help with getting the room ready, particularly sharpening pencils to use at the tables. A listening center was set up so children could hear some words about worship. Psalm 100 was on the tape with two voices reading antiphonally. Because the session was built around the idea of group action there were no individual choices of learning centers.

There was an action card for every child with a different picture on each card. (See Illustration A.) Because we had sixteen children we had four different colors for the action cards. These four colors formed the basis for grouping. Children were free to trade once they had done what the card told them to do. Then, at a signal from the piano, "color" teams were formed and the four children in each team arranged their actions as the group was to follow them. Each "color" team lined up before the group and displayed the "order of action." (Main Idea #1.)

After the group settled down, we discussed the experience. What was it like when each person was doing his or her own thing? What was it like when we got together? Why is a plan important when several people want to do something? The leader showed the plan the people of God follow (the bulletin). She explained that the minister and leaders of the church usually made this plan and they used the Bible to guide them. (Main Ideas #2, 3, 7.)

Illustration A: Action Cards

The leaders displayed four large worship action cards with pictures. (See Illustration B.) They emphasized the verbs and read each sentence clearly. Then the children received a set of four cards. They studied them, and suggested ways of arranging the cards on the bulletin board so we could follow them. (Main Idea #4.)

The leader displayed the bulletin again and said this was like our worship action cards. It was a plan of action without pictures. The children went to tables in small groups to study the bulletin. First they counted the number of separate acts in the bulletin (usually around 18 to 20 acts). They numbered these. Then the leader of each group would match a worship action card with a number. Or a child would ask, "What is number 4?" (Main Ideas #5, 6.)

Remaining in small groups, the children contributed to the total group summary. They observed how many things there were to do; how many words there were; and that it was a good idea to have some "rules" to go by. The leader said our ideas about worship are given to us by God. We already have heard some of these plans. You may even know some of them by memory. The leader then read Psalm 100 and closed with prayer. (Main Idea #7.) The children received a study sheet for worship to use that day that reinforced their work on the bulletin. (See Illustration C.)

Worship Cards: A Design for Studying the Order of Worship in Elementary Grades

In the four years following first grade our children think in new ways. Increasingly they are able to combine facts and draw conclusions in a logical fashion. They see relationships— the whole as well as separate parts. This work of learning, sorting, and combining to create order will occur as they look at the acts of worship that are our response to God.

Second graders still need to step back and look at the separate parts with first graders. But they are capable also of stepping forward to see the attitudes and feelings behind our

Illustration B: Worship Action Cards

1. Open your bulletin.

2. Put a number by each thing we do today.

3. Print this word.

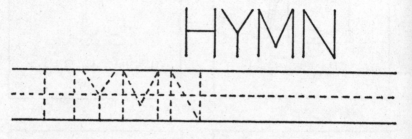

4. Find the word HYMN in the bulletin.

5. Draw a line under HYMN each time you find it.

6. How many did you find? _____

7. Find as many hymns as you can. Mark them in the HYMNBOOK.

8. Stand and hold the HYMNBOOK during the hymn.

Illustration C: Study Sheet for Worship

specific actions. They see that different actions can represent a similar response. They are moving from "how" into "what" and toward "why."

Most sixth grade children move forward into the final stage of their cognitive development. Now they begin to think as most adults do. They begin to go from the very specific and concrete to the general and abstract. They can interpret and evaluate. Now the reason and purpose behind these acts of worship can be examined. The order of worship can represent to them the dynamic life of worship.

Though the way of thinking through these elementary years and our expectations for their learning differs, still a common tool—a set of worship cards—can be used by all six grades, beginning with those who can read some words. Indeed, worship cards can be the basis for a number of intergenerational studies, allowing adults and children to work together to understand congregational worship.

Making Worship Cards

A set of worship cards is made by listing each act in the order of worship on a separate card. The set will also contain special acts of worship: baptism, communion, ordination, installation.

Each card would contain information similar to the examples in Illustration D. For younger children the cards may have simple illustrations.

Each person should have a set of cards. Older children can make their own sets. One way of study would be to place a sentence on the card and let the child print the appropriate act of worship. However, long tedious printing will contribute little to learning in this case. Unless children write well, they should not be burdened with copying and neatness. It is best to make the cards in advance.

Twenty or more cards for each child is an ambitious task if done by hand. The simplest procedure is to mimeograph the cards. (Eight cards can be made from an $8\frac{1}{2}$" $\times$ 11" sheet.) Index cards are usable but require individual typing or printing.

PRELUDE
We prepare to
worship God.

FIRST HYMN
We praise God in
a song.

INVOCATION
We call on God.

PRAYER OF CONFESSION
We say to God:
"I was wrong. I'm sorry."

Illustration D: Worship Cards

The cards are to be handled and will need to withstand wear. Use a good quality paper, cover these sheets with clear plastic, and then cut them. Or make the cards by using a laminating machine.

Using Worship Cards
The following activities are a few that can be developed from the set of cards. Children and teachers alike can think of others. The activities can be used in study units on worship, choir studies, broadly graded extended sessions, and intergenerational experiences. They may even prove useful to parents, worship committees, and pastors.

1. *Arrange the Cards in Order.* A bulletin or printed order of worship should be before the group. People may work in pairs or alone. The object is to become familiar with our acts of worship.

2. *Arrange the Cards as a Temporary Bingo Board.* Here the order is random, but as cards are drawn and called out the worship words become familiar. Cards may be turned over when they are called.

3. *Musical Walk.* Tape the cards around the top of a long table. The children walk around the table, touching each card as they pass by. When the music stops, each child acts out the action listed on his or her card. If a child cannot do it, he or she drops out. The last one standing wins.

4. *Charades.* Divide into two sides. One player from each team draws a card and dramatizes what it represents while the team tries to guess. They can keep the card if they are correct. The side with the most cards wins.

5. *Crazy Eights or Wild Cards.* This game is played like the card game Crazy Eights. The object is to get rid of all your cards by placing them down in sequence. The four special acts of worship (baptism, communion, ordination, installation) are wild cards and can be played in any sequence. One set of

worship cards is needed for every two players. The first player to the left of dealer who has "Prelude" puts it face up. Another player follows with the next act in the bulletin. The game moves more quickly if a large copy of the order of worship is on an easel or bulletin board. This should be removed in later rounds of the game.

These first five suggestions are all ways of building vocabularly through word hearing and usage, and becoming familiar with the sequence of events in worship. The last game is too difficult for first graders. Teachers can help first and second graders with words in the first four without slowing up the game.

6. *Times in Worship.* This game can be played by children working as individuals or pairs. The object of the game is to accumulate points by putting out the most cards when a category is called. To put out a card that does not fit in the category subtracts points. In this version of the game the cards are returned to the player at the end of each category. The categories may be placed on cards to be drawn, or they may be called out by a teacher or made up by the children. Some categories could be: times in the service when we stand, times when we are sitting down, times when we pray, times when we sing, times when we use hymnbooks, times when we praise, times when we give, times when we pray silently, etc.

The game moves more quickly if the object is to get rid of all the cards. Here the cards are not returned to the player and no score is kept. A wrong card must be returned to the owner's stack and a penalty card picked up from the cards played.

This game and the ones that follow are for children third grade and beyond. The older they become the more sophisticated becomes their reasoning for including a subject in a certain category. Obviously one part of the worship service can be included in several categories. Occasionally a sixth grader will justify every card going down on "a time of prayer." The leader has to act as judge in this case. Having the players explain their reasons for playing certain cards makes the game worthwhile.

7. *God Speaks—We Answer.* One way of looking at the worship service is to say it is a conversation between God and us. God began the conversation long ago when he called Abraham and continued it by sending Jesus and calling us into the church. Now let the children in pairs divide the acts of worship into times when God speaks and times when we answer.

8. *Bible Study of Worship.* Read Isaiah 6:1–9a or Luke 5:1–11. This passage is a story about an experience of worship. Answer the following:

The time of the event was _____
The place of the event was _____
What happened? (I saw the Lord, etc.) _____
A feeling: _____
Find a worship card that matches this.

9. *Defining Worship.*
—Arrange your worship cards before you.
—Think about this statement about worship: *The purpose of worship is to praise God, enjoy God's presence, and hear God's word.*
—Do you think this is a true statement? a good statement?
—Now look at your set of worship cards. Select those which help you praise, enjoy, and hear.
—Do any cards not meet these requirements for worship? Why not?
—What will you leave out if this is your definition of worship? What will you add?
—Place your cards in front of you so we can compare.

10. *Planning Worship.* You are responsible for planning worship. The following events (listed on worship cards) occur each Sunday, and on occasion four special events occur (indicate cards for baptism, communion, ordination, installation).
—Arrange the events first in the order that shows what is most meaningful to what is least meaningful to you in worship.
—Compare your arrangement with another person's.

—Now join with this person in planning for worship.
—Can you agree on what to include?
—Can you agree on what to exclude?
—Can you agree on the order in which the events occur?
—When you disagreed, how did you make your decision?
—Who plans our worship each Sunday?
—How do they decide?

Activities 8 and 9 are for older children, especially sixth graders.

7 Leading Children into Worship Through Music

Music and children are a natural combination. Sound and rhythm, the basic musical building blocks, fascinate even a baby. We sing to children long before they can talk, communicating comfort, peace, happiness, and companionship. As they grow they delight in the pulse of the cement mixer, savor the tone of clanging spoon or whistling bird, and accompany their play and games with chants. Barring physical handicap or adult intervention, children will respond to music and express themselves in musical form.

Music and worship are a natural combination too. Music is an ideal medium for addressing God and expressing our needs and hopes before God. We are involved physically, mentally, and emotionally and united in one voice through a hymn. Every aspect of worship can be set to music or interpreted through music.

We are commanded to come into God's presence with singing. From the song of triumph at the exodus to the chorus of the new Jerusalem, God's people are a singing people. Count the times music is used in your own church's service. The number will be an impressive testimony to the role music plays in worship.

In music, then, we have an important and powerful link between the lives of children and the response of worship. We want to do all we can to strengthen this natural link and extend the child's understanding and experience of worship through it. How can we do this? Will any use of music accomplish this? Will all hymns enable children to offer the response of genuine praise and thanksgiving? When our primary concern is not simply to have a happy experience singing but a deeper experience worshiping, how shall we use music? And how shall we involve children in its use?

When music leads children into worship its use is directed by our theology.

We cannot remind ourselves too frequently that God is the beginning and end of worship. Music is always a means to the end of glorifying and enjoying God.

This is easier to state than to practice. Often we choose hymns not to give voice to our praise but because we like them, we know them, or we want variety in our service. We select service music, not to prepare us for worship, but to display the talents of the organist. The choir sings an anthem, not because it speaks an appropriate word from God, but because they have it ready.

Congregational ability and taste, the accompanist's talents, and the choir's preparation are all factors in our selection, but they ought not to be the determining factors. The purpose of worship tests all we do musically in a corporate service.

When music leads children into worship it is a congregational response.

It is not difficult to see hymns as a congregational activity. Some people do stand and wait, enduring patiently until the "amen." This is seldom held up as model conduct or the best use of the time. Though we are sometimes guilty of singing without thought, we understand these words to be our prayers and praise offered to God.

It is more difficult to see that choral and instrumental music involve congregational response as well. We listen to this music as spectators or critics when actually we are participants offering and receiving. Service music is not played to create a mood or to entertain; it is an aid to participation or an expression of participation. The soloist's words are our words to God. The anthem is received as God's word to us. The organ prelude may be a statement of the joy or peace of the Christian life, expressing for us our praise and thanksgiving.

Practicing these two principles has a number of effects in the church's life. Hymns are carefully selected with both verbal and musical content in mind. The hymnbook reflects the theology we profess and the full range of subjects we need for expressing and interpreting our liturgy. Musical leadership contributes to the planning for worship and serious attention is given to their training in worship. Leaders of worship will invest time and energy in enabling the congregation to sing. There will be intentional education about music. The most important single effect, however, will be an attitude. Each person will feel his or her voice is a valued instrument for praising God and will feel capable as well as responsible for responding to God musically. Stewardship of voice rather than display of talent will be the emphasis.

Music that is a valid part of worship spills over into the daily life of the congregation. Hymns sung in worship sustain, express, and inform our faith throughout the week. Children who live in such a congregation will inevitably sing. This is partly because such music is contagious. It is also because they are part of a congregation that enables members to sing.

What does enabling children to sing involve? Our first thought may be a children's choir, and we will think about the role of choirs next. The beginning step, however, is helping children to sing as members of the congregation. More than merely exposing them to music they can hear in worship, we can select hymns with their needs before us and deliberately educate them in the use of the hymnbook.

Selecting Hymns with Children in Mind

Dismiss at once the idea this means only "Jesus Loves Me" or a chorus with a catchy tune. With help children can learn to sing almost all the hymns the congregation sings. A well edited hymnbook already has eliminated tunes that require too wide a vocal range or demand octave leaps in one measure. One syllable to a note is the usual pattern and this is the pattern children need. In short, hymn tunes have been selected because they are singable; and what the congregation can sing, children can sing. We are not concerned here with accuracy of pitch and beauty of tone, but simply with the melody being within the abilities of the singer.

Hymn vocabulary and ideas cause more difficulty. We laughingly relate stories about "Sweet land of liver tea" and "Round John Virgin." One three-year-old sang with vigor, "and heaven and not you sing." Though her version of "Joy to the World" excluded some from participating, she knew the intent of the song—rejoicing in Christ's birth. When the context is understood, vocabulary eventually expands. No child or adult can explain fully the Trinity, but both can offer honest praise through "Holy, Holy, Holy."

An important guide in choosing hymns for children is the use of repeated phrases. "Alleluia" is repeated in each phrase of "Praise the Lord, His Glories Show," and any four- or five-year-old can sing half the song automatically if we simply suggest they join at that place in the hymn. "When Morning Gilds the Skies," "All Hail the Power of Jesus' Name," "Jesus Christ Is Risen Today," and "Come, Christians, Join to Sing" are examples of hymns children can sing in part without reading or extensive vocabulary. These are worthy hymns for adults as well. Including one hymn with easily identified phrases in each worship service is not a severely restricting guideline.

Many hymns do have comprehensible thoughts for children, and they are not childish. Cecil Frances Alexander wrote her words to interpret the Apostles' Creed for children. "All Things Bright and Beautiful," "Once in Royal David's City," and "There Is a Green Hill Far Away" are valid theological statements made simply and without condescension.

When we provide education for the congregation in using hymns and listening to service music, children will be included in this naturally. Occasional bulletin inserts defining words or explaining a hymn theme can be printed. One church displayed pictures interpreting certain hymns, and one sponsored an all-church night for illustrating hymns.

A hymn of the month is an excellent device for helping

children learn music with the congregation. At a worship committee meeting a high school girl requested the church return to the practice of learning a new hymn by singing it for four Sundays either as part of the service or in a pre-service congregational rehearsal. "That was the way I learned to sing," she said, "and I knew everyone was learning just like me."

Without drastically changing repertoire or excluding adults we can select hymns that fit children's abilities.

Helping Children Use the Hymnbook

We can also offer specific help in using the hymnbook. We can encourage every family to have one and can consider presenting a hymnbook to children as they begin to read, just as we present Bibles. We want children to handle hymnbooks and feel they are valuable, useful possessions.

Before children can read they can count. We need to provide them with bookmarks, help them locate hymns, and put them to work counting stanzas and page numbers. Before they can read and as beginning readers they can recognize repeated phrases, the "amen" at the end of the hymn, and the page arrangement: title, subject, music, and words.

As children learn to read, we need to encourage them to use this skill in relation to the hymnbook. Every hymn contains "a," "an," and "the"; suggest to a child that he or she find them. The first grader who learns to read "dog" surely can locate and read "God." Children do need help in moving their eyes across the line of words beneath the music. Words are divided or extended to match musical notes and we move from one line of music to the next rather than to the next line of print. This means an adult must use the bookmark to help children follow the words until they learn the method. In an enabling congregation, parents and other adults will feel comfortable doing just this. There will be no sense of interrupting worship or being disrespectful.

As children grow they need help in understanding the arrangement of the hymnbook. They want to be able to find hymns, responses, and worship aids for themselves. The hymn itself is surrounded by information that can make the hymnbook a source of interest: author, composer, dates, translators, original sources, and meters.

After church one Sunday, Karl, a lively sixth grade boy, invited his teacher to a school performance of HMS Pinafore. "I'm going to be the admiral," he announced proudly.

"I hope you practiced well when you sang Mr. Sullivan's music this morning," said his friend.

"We didn't sing anything from HMS Pinafore this morning, did we?" was Karl's puzzled question. And the adult and child sat down together to locate all of Arthur Sullivan's hymn tunes in the composer's index at the back of the hymnbook.

"I didn't know real people wrote for hymnbooks," was Karl's remark as he counted the melodies again.

Such education, planned or casual, will help children develop understanding as well as skill in singing. The hymnbook has come from the life of other Christians to us, and we join a choir transcending space and time when we sing.

Leading Children to Worship Through Choirs

Many churches educate children in music through choirs. This has not always been the church's pattern. Though the church has used boys' unchanged voices for centuries, children's choirs as we know them have developed since 1900.[17] The growth of the church junior choir program has been phenomenal.

Now choirs for children come in all ages and sizes. One church combines a dozen children from kindergarten through seventh grade while others divide three hundred young people into a system of closely graded groups from preschool through high school. Some churches have handbells, instruments, a practice room, a library of music, and a full array of cottas and surplices. Others work enthusiastically with hymnbooks and the instructions, "Everybody wear a white shirt or blouse."

In general we may applaud the church's concern for teaching children to sing. Though congregational understanding and use of music have primary impact on the child's life of worship, choirs can make an enormous contribution in children's worship growth. Not every choir does this. The next two episodes of choir organization may help us see why.

The Westbend Church

At the Westbend Church's summer picnic several parents were talking after supper.

"We visited Trinity Church last week," said Lyn Vanetta. "They have the most active children's choir. They must have thirty members. Even Ben perked up when he noticed one of the boys playing a drum. And they looked so cute in those bright robes—like little angels even when you knew they were little devils."

"I don't see why we can't have a choir for our children," remarked Nat Palmer. "We have enough youngsters in the park right now to form a group. Our girls need something to keep them interested. They're the only children in our neighborhood who go to church."

"They might even hook a few of the children in the neighborhood into coming if they sing music with a little pep that young people like," added Ruth Palmer.

There was general agreement that a choir would be a good thing. The minister responded to the suggestion; the worship committee approved; and several interested parents began a choir that fall.

The project was enthusiastically received. By Christmas they had a director and robes. Several gifts made it possible to buy music. The year ended with more children in the group than had enrolled at the beginning. They celebrated with two special songs at the morning worship, a closing picnic, and more ambitious plans for the next year.

The Salem Falls Church

In a more formal setting a committee of the Salem Falls Church interviewed a director of youth choirs. The 2,000 member church planned to expand their two choirs into a comprehensive music program for children from three through high school age.

"We need lots of community building experiences for our young people," began Mrs. Lenz. "We're a downtown church and these young folks need to get to know each other and have a good time together."

"I'm impressed with your vocal training," said Arthur Hedges. "We want our children to sing well. We have the best adult choir in town and we want the same high standards for our children. A quality music program attracts members besides providing good music for the church service."

"We've found whenever children do something in church the parents always come. We have to give them something to do if we want to get the disinterested ones here," contributed Paula Glanzer. "People have to have a good reason to be here before they'll drive from the suburbs into town."

"But they don't need to sing too often," interrupted Mrs. Lenz. "We're so close to the capitol we have many visitors each Sunday. Children can be a distraction in the choir, especially if they don't know how to behave. And I think people really want to hear good music like the adult choir sings. It is good to have the children sing on Christmas and Easter."

"I'd like to see them sing every Sunday," said Arthur Hedges. "It makes me feel good just to see all those cute little ones up there. Everyone likes to see the children in church."

The prospective minister of music pondered the job description. On the plus side he listed strong interest and support, adequate financing, and a large number of children and young people. In the negative side he noted, "conflicting expectations."

Two things stand out in these situations. The first is the mixed aims that lie behind many choirs—fellowship, evangelism, parental satisfaction, music education, and congregational entertainment are only a few. Some of these are worthy goals. Any choir director in church or community hopes for fellowship, increased interest, and responsible participation. Good musical development is the desire of all who work with children in choirs.

And it should be noted here that excellent resources are available for any director who wants to train children's voices wisely and select their music well. Several of these are listed in the bibliography. The problem is not so much with good aims as it is with conflicting aims.

The second observation is this: the purposes for which the choirs in the two episodes were organized had little to do with the use made of the choirs. The primary area of service in both instances was assumed to be contributing music in congregational worship. The objectives around which the choirs were developed had little to do with that.

The child who sings in either of the two organizations we have just observed will learn a number of things that actually hinder a sense of God's presence and oneness with God's people. This child could conclude:

> I am cute. People like to see me sing.
> How I sing is less important than how I look.
> How I sing is more important than why I sing.
> I am the focus of worship. Worship is only important to me and my parents when I am "doing something" in the service.
> I perform well when I do not distract anyone.
> I worship at Christmas and Easter.

When we expect choirs for children and youth to contribute to worship then we must articulate this intent as clearly as possible. An understanding of worship and education for worship must be built into the program. The choir will be both a learning experience and an avenue of service, but it will never be a performance group.

Characteristics of the Worship-Oriented Choir

A worship-oriented approach requires constant support and interpretation. Parents and grandparents who come to church "because Denise is singing" need some tactful education. Congregations that wish alternately to view cherubic choirs and to eliminate demonic behavior need help with their expectations. Ministers and worship planners who consider youth choirs only as the icing on a festival cake need their horizons broadened. Choir directors who emphasize musical perfection over learning and contribution need assurance that they are not on trial. "Singing our best," always a goal, need not mean a perfectly polished anthem.

Commitment to worship is a first consideration in securing choir leadership. Knowledgeable persons responsible for planning worship can maintain contact with the director, and the director can have some part in worship planning.

An understanding of choir purpose can be built into recruitment. Children can be invited into a serious but joyful discipline. Their purpose is to lead the congregation in worship through music. In the process they must not only sing but also pray, listen, and confess their faith in creed and hymn.

The music they sing can make a legitimate contribution to the worship service. It can be judged by the same theological standards as any other music in the service. Children need to know just how their music will enable persons to worship and some of the reasons a particular song was chosen. Theirs is not a haphazard offering but a carefully planned, purposeful gift.

In a worship-oriented choir participants have additional opportunities to know and understand the order of worship and the part they play in these actions. They can learn and can use the responses that are part of their regular worship—the Lord's Prayer, the creeds, the Doxology, Gloria, and other musical responses.

This direction does not eliminate joy, friendship, outreach, or the personal development of each child. To worship God means to offer God our best. We want the highest level of musical training and knowledge possible. We want to offer leaders encouragement and support in seeking additional training and skill for themselves. Music is too powerful a force and children's voices are too valuable a gift to suffer because of poor leadership.

But a choir that is to contribute to worship must be educated in worship, and this education must be intentionally built into the choir program.

The following is a suggested outline of goals for a youth choir program:

I. *A good youth choir program will lead into worship.*

Through a knowledge of the purpose, elements, and order of worship gained through opportunities to worship and lead in worship.

Through an understanding of the place of music in worship.

Through increasing skill in using resources of worship, particularly the hymnbook.

II. *A good youth choir program will lead into music.*

Through exposure to a wide range of good music.

Through development in music literacy.

Through development in vocal and instrumental proficiency.

III. *A good youth choir program will lead into the heritage of the Christian faith.*

Through the theological and devotional content of good texts.

Through the history of the music sung.

Through the knowledge of the church year and participation in services celebrating these events in Christ's life.

IV. *A good youth choir program will lead into personal growth.*

Through opportunities for service.

Through assuming responsibilities.

Through an understanding of the stewardship of talents.

V. *A good youth choir program will lead into community.*

Through cooperation with leaders and other choirs.

Through contributions to the life of the church.

Through responsible commitment to the group.

8 Planning for Children in Worship

Who Does the Planning?

The pastor does the planning for worship, of course! This broad assumption is true but not true enough. Certainly the pastor of a congregation conducts the services of worship, preaches, leads the prayers, and administers the sacraments. All this requires careful, dedicated planning and preparation. Much of what happens in a worship service depends on the faithfulness of the pastor in planning, based on his or her knowledge of the theology and traditions of worship and understanding of the spirit of this central activity of the church.

But worship is a corporate act. The congregation participates not only in its weekly celebration but also in planning and preparing for worship. Worship is too important to be left to the experts. All must be involved, for all participate and are deeply affected by it. Small congregations or house churches are at great advantage in that they easily can organize teams of church members to plan and conduct worship. There probably is no better way to ensure the inclusion of the life and concerns of the people into each service of worship. The educational possibilities are endless in such a program. Members learn about God's grace and the ways in which they can respond as they discuss each week the ways in which they will worship God. Every church can consider such a way to plan worship. But for most churches, particularly those with two hundred or more members, worship usually is planned or at least supervised by a worship committee.

The worship committee usually is advised by the pastor and is responsible to the church council or session. It communicates with other committees and groups to coordinate education, evangelism, and the many other facets of church life with the central act of worship. In whatever way a committee is chosen, the church is well-served if it selects persons who are open-minded, willing to learn, and sensitive to the concerns of other members. While these characteristics are ideal for any committee, they are particularly suited for the demands of the worship committee. More than one church has been ill-served by worship committee members who already know what worship is, ought to be, and will forever remain. More often than not, such rigid notions lock in on worship habits rather than on truly traditional and responsible theological understandings of worship. Especially for the sake of the children a worship committee needs to be filled with persons who look at worship theologically and will create worship practices that are appropriate for all the current members of the church. For example, such a person would be willing and happy to consult with a ten-year-old member of the church to find out how worship is perceived by this child.

The precise role definition for a worship committee is based on its denominational directory for worship and on local congregational structure. The Continuum for Role Definition illustrates a way that a worship committee can educate itself about its tasks through a discussion of the answers. Pastors and committee chairpersons can devise other similar methods for helping committees to learn their roles and responsibilities.

CONTINUUM FOR ROLE DEFINITION

Under each statement place a mark to indicate your current understanding or opinion.

1. The *Book of Church Order* assigns responsibility for planning worship to the session. Ordinarily this is done through a worship committee.

Agree —————————————————————————— *Disagree*

2. Providing the facilities, equipment, and supplies for worship is the most important job of the worship committee.

Agree —————————————————————————— *Disagree*

3. All elements of worship (hymns, prayers, sermons, offerings, etc.) are of equal importance; one should not overshadow another.

Agree —————————————————————————— *Disagree*

4. The worship committee should determine the order of worship together with the pastor.

Agree —————————————————————————— *Disagree*

5. It is important that the worship committee explore different ways of worshiping that reflect changing needs and circumstances of the congregation.

Agree —————————————————————————— *Disagree*

6. The worship committee works with the music director in planning music for worship.

Agree —————————————————————————— *Disagree*

7. It is the worship committee's responsibility to determine when and how special services of worship are observed.

Agree —————————————————————————— *Disagree*

8. The *Book of Church Order* states that children should sit with their families during worship.

Agree —————————————————————————— *Disagree*

A worship committee works with whatever goals are established by a congregational planning process as well as goals determined by the committee itself. Committee members may decide, for example, that they need to heighten their own awareness of the meaning of worship, and then embark on a campaign to help the entire congregation grapple with the meaning. Another goal might be to help adults in the congregation to understand how children perceive worship. Whatever the goals it is helpful for the committee to experience the heady exhilaration of accomplishment. So it would be a smart strategy to include in the committee's work some limited, short-range projects which have a high possibility for immediate success. Putting it plainly, let the committee do something! There will be plenty of long, arduous struggles as the committee works toward a truly worshiping community. They will be encouraged in their efforts by knowing that they have already garnered some accomplishments: made some changes in the room arrangements of the sanctuary, begun a column in the newsletter concerning worship, provided lectionaries and lists of hymns for church school teachers, put into the church budget a scholarship for choir school, established a rotation system for members to bake bread for communion.

The worship committee can claim rightfully that worship is the central, unifying act of the congregation. This is the activity in which all members participate in common, and which joins the congregation in the stream of spiritual unity with the church in all places and at all times. Such a broad perspective calls for attention to the need for coordination between the committee and all the staff, committees, and groups of the church.

A key relationship is with the pastor or pastoral team, as the case may be. The pastor is the primary biblical theologian and church historian for the congregation. He or she fulfills a priestly function and also seeks to preserve the values of the church's tradition. Church polity is also taught and interpreted by the pastor. The worship committee depends on the pastor to teach it and to provide expert leadership and resourcing. Ideally the pastor is the key supporter of the worship committee's visions for the worship of the church and the key implementer of its decisions.

Sometimes pastors' visions for worship look forward while those of the parishioners look backward. Sometimes parishioners cry for change while pastors securely hold on to a repetition of habit. More will be said later about creating a climate for corporate, inclusive worship. In dealing with relationships and coordination let it be said here that pastors and committees alike need to act on the basis of biblical, historical, and denominational standards for worship. In dealing with what can be a highly personal, emotional, and subjective issue the committee must ground its work on the rock of theology. It behooves the committee to be trained in the theology and tradition of worship, perhaps even training itself if the pastor cannot provide this. (See the resources listed in the bibliography.)

Committee members should be slow to fault a pastor or to castigate a congregation for what it considers resistance to change. Change in worship is not sufficiently justified if it is based only on personal preference or "for the sake of the children." Pastor and committee together need to study what worship is and plan for worship which glorifies God and thus serves the needs of the people, whose primary need is to be able to relate with God. Change takes place in the context of the need for ways to respond to God's call to worship.

Another key relationship for the worship committee is with the committee charged with the nurture and education of church members. In regards to children and worship the latter committee can inform the former about child development, how persons are nurtured, what is being done with children in the church, and how worship is being enhanced in various educational settings such as church school and youth groups. There is so much correlation between these two committees that they may want to structure some permanent liaison functions, such as sharing of committee minutes and reports and sharing membership.

The worship committee needs to be in touch with those who work with children in the church. Choir directors, church school teachers, club leaders, and others can inform the committee about what is happening with children and can be informed by the committee concerning how they can contribute to the children's capacities for worship. Learning how to pray, for instance, calls for coordinated efforts on the part of many groups in the church. If worship is to be the central act of the church the worship committee must lead the way in scheduling worship and emphasizing its importance.

Especially during the first five or six years of a child's life the parents are the primary teachers of worship for the child. Most parents want to do a good job of this and will appreciate very much all the help a worship committee (and Christian education committee) can provide. Other chapters in this book give examples of parent education; this form of ministry can be coordinated by the worship committee.

It is not said in jest that the worship committee must be open to consultations with a ten-year-old child. Adults think differently than do children, and often they forget how children perceive worship and participate in it. A committee may want to have two children as members. Or it may want to co-opt children when it at least needs to listen to children—to consult with them—as it decides on matters which affect children.

Creating a Climate for Inclusive Worship

Climate is familiar to us and we understand that life and growth are profoundly affected by it. Small and beautiful mountain wildflowers grow according to what the alpine climate permits; cacti of the desert grow in ways that are allowed by the hot, dry climate of their existence. Wildflowers and cacti alike adapt to the climate. Their roots and leaves take in whatever nutrients they can by adapting their form and function to the climatic limits of sun, air, water, and soil. We can think of worshipers in a similar relationship to the climate in which they live, grow, and worship. To meet a worshiper whose concept of worship is one of joyful celebration suggests that she has been blessed with a climate for worship in her congregation that encourages thanksgiving, happiness, and expressiveness. A more "desert-like climate" may lead a worshiper to a dryness of soul and spirit, suggesting a barrenness and austerity of worship form and expression.

At a workshop on including children in worship two participants, John Cairns and Greg Funfgeld, offered a list of elements of congregational "climate" as legitimate expectations of the worshiping community. Consider how this list can spur the thinking of a worship committee:

—That no one should be bored.

—That all our senses should be involved and our faculties developed.

—That our baptismal commitment to each other should be actualized.

—That all participants should have the opportunity to contribute.

—That persons are able to receive gifts from each other.

—That worshipers can be a source of surprise and spontaneous inspiration for each other.

—That vulnerability should be necessary.

—That signs and imagery should be developed corporately and shared so that worshipers may grow in faith.

—That faith should be transmitted through rituals and the input of previous generations.

—That elements of worship such as prayer and praise are an essential part of the daily life of all Christians.

—That attention should be given to the level of understanding of each member of the worshiping community.

In offering this list Cairns and Funfgeld understood a corporate church—faithful members of the body whose head is Christ. The attitudes and characteristics listed above describe a climate very conducive to worship which is corporate, inclusive, personal, spontaneous, lively, and faithful.

Much of this kind of climate (or whatever climate a church desires) is established during worship. It follows that a worshiping community which pays attention to personal growth and life events, and which provides frequent occasions for personal commitment and renewal of dedication, will help establish a congregation where individual members feel wanted, needed, recognized, and challenged. In so many ways the spirit of worship sets the tone for the spirit of the congregation.

The converse is also true. Worship will reflect the tone and attitudes of the congregation and its life. If we suppose a congregation and pastor that has become enthusiastic about the value of children in their midst, we could expect action on behalf of the children. Programming for children will increase, but so will activities which put children and older persons together. Efforts will be made to speak to children, with due consideration for styles and methods of communication, such as the use of simple, direct language. Adults will learn from children, recreating in themselves a sense of fantasy, spontaneity, or mystery. Storytelling will once again be a way of sharing faith; thanksgiving will emphasize again a sense of dependence and interdependence. Were these ideal characteristics to be the climate within a congregation, one would feel an excited sense of expectancy about the nature and quality of its worship.

Church members need to learn again—to be reformed— concerning the relationship between faith and life and worship. The happiness or the searching doubt which they sense in life must be allowed to be expressed in worship. Community and mutual care must find its expression in worship too. Determination and dedication need to be expressed. The pastor and the worship committee can be sensitive to this "spirit" of the congregation and plan creatively to allow this spirit to be expressed—to be brought before God for sanctification and transformation. Then worship truly will be sincere worship in spirit and in truth for the people.

Climate can be recognized and, to a great degree, adjusted. There are large concerns to be recognized, such as enabling a community of people to understand themselves to be called by God into covenant relationship. Preaching, teaching, worship, counseling, and every other aspect of congregational life must be devoted to the imparting of this kind of understanding of the identity and nature of the people. In addition to the larger aspects of church life myriad smaller aspects can contribute to the adjustment of climate. Teaching and interpreting take place through the weekly newsletter. Similar nurture takes place during worship, such as when the worship leader asks the congregation to share its concerns for specific persons so that intercessory prayers can be offered on their behalf. Using church suppers also as times for learning to sing hymns contributes to a church's climate. Observing the church year and seasons in all departments will also contribute. So will the encouraging and resourcing of small group worship and the using of the lectionary for personal and group study. In many ways a worship committee and pastor can create a climate for inclusive worship.

One way for setting a climate deserves special mention: family worship. Families that worship together will support the church's efforts for its "family" to worship together. When parents and children pray, sing, and read scripture together, they develop attitudes toward worship which tend to be corporate, spontaneous, and respectful of personal sharing. These attitudes are beneficial to the congregation's worship. In every way possible the worship committee should encourage family worship. Resources can be provided, and constant exhorting is needful. But perhaps the most helpful way in this day is that of providing models of what can be done by families. Modern families have scant experience of bedtime prayers, mealtime graces, joint reading of scripture, and family or home centered celebrations of religious holidays and personal milestones. Such models may be introduced in neighborhood gatherings, pastoral visits, parents groups, and similar events.

But the old piety of personal and family devotions may

need to be supplanted with different motivations. In the recent past personal prayer and devotional life were called for to fulfill religious duty or to express personal piety. It would be better to understand that personal and family worship are extensions of corporate worship. Because we are members of the covenant community, the body of Christ, we worship together. And because of this same identity as members of the community we also worship as individuals. Indeed, much of the material of corporate worship is resource for personal worship. Every home should have a hymnbook, prayerbooks, and lectionary, so that what is celebrated corporately extends into the home and is continued there. Further, let it be understood that families worship together in order to praise God in response to God's grace and mercy. In a child's terms, we worship at home because we want to thank God for all that God is and has done for us. We do not "do devotions" in order to please God and to gain favor. And while much learning takes place as we pray with children, we do not pray in order to teach them to pray. Prayer and worship are means for responding to God. The learning that takes place is significant but is secondary. In the end, for children to understand that worship is something we do to praise God, rather than something we do in order to learn, is a great accomplishment.

Being Sensitive to Feelings

A wise pastor emeritus once oriented a new, young pastor to the congregation by telling him to beware of the War Department of the church. What was meant was the choir. What the wise old man lost in accuracy he gained in emphasis, for he was right in implying that when it comes to worship, as to artistic expression, people get very emotional. Worship committees and pastors beware too! It may be easier for a camel to squeeze through the eye of a needle than for certain changes to be made in worship.

Persons who seek to make changes need to be armed with no less than theological integrity, "due patience," the wisdom of a serpent, flexibility, and the ability to do good educational and interpretive work.

On the one hand, change must be theologically responsible; on the other hand, any change may disturb someone's sense of security and propriety. As pointed out earlier, what may prove most feasible is to introduce a new practice without removing an old one. A pastor may preach so that children are included in the sermon, while still conducting "A Time with the Younger Church." In time the latter practice may outlive its usefulness and people will be glad to see it go. One church added the practice of having the people come forward to receive the bread and wine of communion, but did not remove the practice of serving bread and wine to people seated in the pews. They simply alternated practices each month. Several years of continuing both practices has surprised all parties with the pleasure and variety of sharing bread and wine in more than one way. In this case it seemed that everyone won and no one lost. It might have been different if the older method had been thrown out.

Worship leaders help educate worshipers when they explain why certain actions are taken during worship. A minister who stands at the communion table to lead in the people's prayer could educate simply by saying, "As we gather together around the Table of our Lord, let us offer the prayers of our community . . . ." Or the printed order of worship may explain, "Hymn of Praise," or "Gloria Patri: We praise the Holy Trinity for the message of the Bible."

Worship is a serious matter. Its centrality in the life of the church is unquestioned. Its content addresses the concerns of every member of the church, young and old alike. In its best practice worship is deeply emotional. So those who would plan worship or change its form or practice must do so out of a true love for the church and a sincere desire to enable the church to praise God. Theological integrity must be matched with sensitivity to the human aspects of worship, and decisions made with wisdom and love.

Some frank words to pastors bring this chapter to a close.

Everything which has been said to the worship committee concerning integrity and sensitivity is meant for pastors too. The issue of including children in worship is initially an issue of the nature of corporate worship. Worship is for all the church members to do; it is not a performance by a trained and dramatic worship leader. Borrowing Sören Kierkegaard's metaphor, we are reminded that in worship God is the audience and we are the actors or players; a minister may be a play director, which merely accentuates a servant role. For all the import that accrues to the priestly function, it is still a mediating role to enable people and God to relate. Pastors serve well when they see in their worship committee leadership opportunities for ministry. Worship is for the pastor a form of ministry.

9 How a Pastor Relates to the Children

Yes, Virginia, there is a Santa Claus, and yes, Virginia, a pastor can relate to children. Most already do. Some feel a lack of confidence or lack of know-how. A few pastors share W. C. Fields' approach: "No man who hates children and dogs could be all bad." The goal of this book is to show to all in the church, even those harboring some malice toward children, that children are members of the church and belong in its corporate worship. Crucial to the actualization of this ideal is the pastor. This chapter tells of one pastor's attempts to minister to children and then offers specific suggestions for all pastors.

Keith and the Kids

The Rev. Keith Huggins was three years out of seminary when he, a former all-conference lineman with hulking body to back up the image, found himself becoming more and more sensitive to children as persons. In his parish there were specific children who needed pastoral care. His initial attempts at ministry with children were hit or miss, somewhat like the efforts of a Frankenstein's monster trying to be comfortable picking flowers with an innocent little child. But his heart was in it. Keith made sure he talked with children as well as adults in the church hallways before and after worship. He organized his schedule so that he could be a visiting teacher in the elementary grade classes. He got to know "the kids" pretty well, and they got to know him and could recognize him even when he didn't have his black robe on (which made him look so-o-o big anyway!).

When Keith agreed to be the subject of a seminary student's project, the pieces fell in place. What was a trial and error, hit or miss attempt at ministry with children began to be guided by a rationale and strategy. Regular consultations with the student, Don Cameron, helped Keith to learn the broad outlines of child development. Don's suggestions and questions helped Keith not only to see why he should be doing ministry directly with children, but also how specific acts could be done.

Children, Don loved to say, are persons, not puppies—you don't pat them on the head and say how cute they are; you shake their hands and converse with them. You respect them and try to find out from them what they are thinking about and what issues confront them. Keith learned, by doing, how to talk with children. He found out that a certain child was worried about his parents' divorce, and another child was going to the hospital soon. He was able to affirm children whose birthdays he noted, and he was ready to listen when a child talked about having to move to another town or losing a grandfather.

Keith was realizing more fully the possibilities of the various intergenerational activities of the church, such as potluck suppers, picnics, receptions, stewardship events, and events of the church year. He made sure that children were included as leaders in the Advent rituals on Sunday mornings, and that specific plans were made for them during the otherwise very informal suppers. What he was working toward was a church which would consider it normal to have children genuinely participate in most of its activities.

Infant baptisms became more dramatic and ritualistic. Often all the children in the congregation were invited to gather in the chancel area to witness closely the ritual, and to be the first ones to greet the infant and the parents as they were introduced to the entire congregation. Keith found himself taking more care in counseling with parents, and he saw the value of parents' classes and support groups.

Don also was priming Keith's theological pump, helping Keith to get a handle on the concepts of membership in the body of Christ and mutual ministry with each other. At the same time Keith had the opportunity to attend a synod workshop on confirmation-commissioning. More pieces fell in place as he saw how ministry with children leads to further growth and new decisions and forms of faith and witness for each person. If a person is to be able to articulate a personal commitment and to accept a commissioning to responsible membership, then certain experiences and opportunities for growth were needed during childhood to point to that commitment.

Keith began to see that each child had to experience being a part of the worshiping community. He began to see what each child needed to know about the Christian tradition and the church's mission. Now he could make sense of the church school curriculum, and he was anxious that the teachers and parents be able to see that rationale too.

Keith found himself planning for and leading worship differently. He was aware of the diversity of the congregation, and of their individual needs and interests, and he knew the standards of theology and tradition. Corporate worship was a challenge! Right about this time he moved from behind the pulpit to the communion table when he led worship, and found that not only was he closer to the people, but that he was symbolizing community and participation. Often a call to prayer was begun, "Boys and girls, men and women. . . ." The content of the prayers was more inclusive and addressed the concerns of all kinds of people, including children. Prayers written by the people, including children's groups, were used. Laypersons assumed more leadership in worship, and some of these laypersons were children. (The first Sunday after the church *fathers* agreed that it was fine to have women as ushers the entire team of ushers was women—but now the ushering teams are mixed in age and gender.) In general, worship took on more pace, had more movement, and offered more occasions for congregational participation. It was a bit strange for the congregation, because they were experiencing more informality and participation at the same time that the worship was becoming more formal and traditional!

Keith has since been called to another congregation. His initial efforts at paying more attention to the children and integrating them into worship have not been lost. A task force is working on solidifying the experimental gains and changes begun by a pastor who surprised himself when he showed each child the respect which is due to any person.

Some General Directions for the Pastor

Several general directions emerge from the story of Keith's attempts to be a pastor to the children of his congregation and to involve them in corporate worship.

1. *Recognize that children are persons.* Children are members of a church by baptism (or by being a part of a family with membership). As members they are entitled to the rights and privileges of worship, nurture, pastoral care, and congregational life. Children who are members are also to be called on to contribute, according to their capacity, to the witness and mission of the congregation. Each child is a member and a person.

The church and its leaders have gotten into a centuries-old habit of ignoring children or relegating them to a shelf marked "For Future Use Only." In these last few years society as a whole and the church particularly have come to realize again that each child is a worthy person. Accepting this fact is the foundation for ministry with children and for their full involvement in worship.

2. *Know the children as persons.* Every pastor is aware of how important it is to know parishioners by name and character. Even pastors of thousand-member churches make some kind of effort, usually rather systematic, to get names and faces properly associated, and to treat members as persons. From Keith's example we can take heart. His sincere attempts were awkward at the beginning but became natural and personal with practice. When Keith really respected the children, then

he paid personal attention to each of them. Anita Tomas was not just Mr. and Mrs. Tomas's school age girl; she was Anita, with her own personality and integrity. The more Keith related with her and talked with her, the more firm their relationship became.

3. *Provide pastoral care.* Children have personal needs and crises that call for pastoral care as provided by the pastor. There is much that a minister can do. A pastor can call on the sick or hospitalized. He or she can minister to those who have suffered loss or trauma. If only those who are of a certain age have their needs ministered to, while others such as children are ignored, then priorities and values need to be overturned. This is a hard word for some pastors, for they are already busy. But it remains true that the church through its pastors must provide pastoral care for its children.

Fortunately churches today are developing new forms and styles of pastoral care which do not rely on the availability of only one person or parson. So it is quite possible that a system of pastoral care can be established so that church members minister to one another. The pastor is involved, of course, but personal care is shared and shouldered by many. If such a system is used by a congregation then the pastor needs to ensure that children are included.

4. *Support the leaders of children.* Ministry in the church is shared. A way in which the work is divided up is for the pastor to exercise leadership and to be a teacher and supporter of others who give leadership in specific ways. This support often is given when the pastor enables other leaders to build up a ministry with children. When worship committee members, church school leaders, choir directors, stewardship committee members, and other workers know that the pastor "is for it and will help implement it," then positive changes in the children's favor can happen. Certainly such changes are hard to imagine when the pastor does not care or drops hints of antagonism toward children.

5. *Worship in the context of total ministry.* Doing this or that with children in the church, here and there and in bits and

pieces, will not accomplish the goal of nurture. For children as well as adults what happens in all areas of church life must relate to worship. And everything that happens in worship relates to and influences all of church life. Being aware of children in the hallway calls for being aware of them in worship. And if children are spoken to in worship it would be hypocritical to ignore them in the hallways.

The potential for good is exciting: the positive changes that are made on behalf of children in the worship and life of the congregation can make an impact upon the whole church which is creative and stimulates growth for all.

6. *Allow the children to minister to you.* The example of Keith Huggins testifies to this suggestion. He was enriched in his own personal life. He was motivated to learn and to put into practice some valuable understandings of worship, human development, and the nature of human community. "The pleasure is mine; I've gotten a lot of joy from the kids."

Some Specific Suggestions for the Pastor

Every Sunday some church is discovering a new way to worship God. Many of these ways involve children; this is a time of interest and inventiveness concerning how the church can minister with children. Here are a few suggestions, examples intended to encourage the church to further developments.

1. *Provide a ministry to parents, including those who are expecting the birth of a child.* Help them to help their children to worship.

2. *Learn the names of children and talk with them, addressing them by their names.* Talk without condescension. When you greet them shake their hands rather than patting their heads.

3. *Acknowledge events which are significant for children.* Send them birthday cards, talk with them about moving, or divorce, or illness, or death. Visit them in their homes, telephone them, and chat with them when they are in the church building.

4. See that other adults also relate with children. Involve them in the educational and pastoral care activities described in this book.

5. Incorporate into worship the events and concerns of the children. Use established rituals such as baptism to "deal with what's happening in life," and create new rituals to mark life passages. For example, welcome new members or say goodbye and Godspeed to old members through appropriate rituals.

In the prayers, litanies, sermons, and other worship activities include references to children. Help them to see that worship and life are related.

6. Support the worship committee. Be an advocate for children on that committee. Require that the committee operate from a solid base of theology and tradition so that their innovations will have theological integrity and historical continuity.

7. Help the worship committee (and any other group) with the dynamics of change. Goal setting and planning processes are useful tools, but what also is needed is some wisdom and discretion about how change comes about in an institution. Consider the wisdom of making changes one at a time, and, where possible, only when more than a handful ask for it. When a change is made, avoid throwing out a practice or replacing it with the change. Oftentimes if a change is valid the old practice will die of its own accord.

8. Provide resources for those who plan worship or advocate improvements in the ministry with children. See the bibliography for suggestions of good materials.

9. With the help of the worship committee and church officers set a healthy climate for integrated corporate worship. Identify areas of potential change or reform and establish strategies for bringing about the changes. For example, establish a theologically responsible definition of membership which includes children, and help the entire church to accept that definition. Educate the congregation about the many meanings of the Lord's Supper, and of the appropriateness of children's participation. Enlist the support of parents for worship reforms. Make it possible for children to minister to adults.

Identify potential problems too. Recognize that there are adults who are not comfortable with children. Acknowledge that previous experiences and practices may discourage change, as in the case of children who are accustomed to misbehavior during worship because they have not known any alternative. Acknowledge the risks of moving too quickly or on too large a scale. Changes in worship require opportunities for worshipers to learn the changes.

10. *Exercise care and skill in conducting services of worship.*

a. Be sure all worship is biblical, theological, and has continuity with tradition.

b. Include as much congregational participation as possible, including lay leadership of worship. Where possible, use children as leaders.

c. Seek a balance between traditional language and simpler, understandable vocabulary.

d. Find occasions during worship and at other times to explain worship and terms used in worship, such as "miserable offenders," "collect," "petition," and "pastoral prayer." Incidentally, if it is not possible to explain a term or act of worship, such as to explain what is a "pastoral prayer," then consider whether or not that item really belongs in corporate worship.

e. Maintain an appropriate pace for worship. Enlist the aid of several worshipers to evaluate how the worship leaders are helping the congregation to move from one act to another, how quickly or slowly words are spoken, and how pauses and silence are used.

f. Use physical movement. Both the leaders and the worshipers can be involved in standing up, coming forward, reaching out, and other movements.

g. Use the visual and aural senses, as well as the tactile. The Lord's Supper is an epitome of seeing, hearing, touching, and tasting; it has movement and pace, and has the dramatic power to pull a worshiper into total participation. Many other acts of worship possess similar potential for sensual involvement.

h. Arrange the worship room for optimum congregational involvement and participation. Children tend to be able to participate better when they are seated in front and can see what is taking place. It seems, surprisingly, that other worshipers are less distracted by noise and movement which they can see. What they can hear but not see, such as children fidgeting and bumping into furnishings while seated in the back of the sanctuary, drives them to distraction.

i. Interpret worship activities as actions. As described in chapter 6, help the worshipers to understand that the Assurance of Pardon is "receiving God's forgiveness." The Creed is "standing up and saying together what we believe," and so forth.

j. Involve the children specifically as much as possible as readers, ushers, choral readers, choir singers, and in bringing in the Bible, the bread and wine, the offering, or in gathering to observe closely an infant baptism.

k. Use a personal style of leadership. It is possible at the same time to be formal and personal, and to follow an order but to do so with grace and occasional humor.

l. See Appendix A for other ways to incorporate children into congregational worship.

11. *Include children as a part of the congregation which is addressed in every sermon.* There need be only one sermon a Sunday! Children's sermons cater only to one age group and thus symbolize an unfortunate division of worshipers. Often children's sermons are merely little moralisms that fail to proclaim a gospel of grace. Ministers fall into habits of manipulation; they succumb to the pressure to entertain the children (and the adults), and do so by asking double entendre questions or using clever gimmicks ("object lessons"). A better activity is a time when the children are called forward and some explanation of worship or church life is told simply and directly. However, even such a "Time with the Younger Church" is difficult to justify biblically, traditionally, or by most other standards for judging worship.

What remains appropriate for all worshipers is an emphasis on the Word of God from scripture and interpreted in a sermon. This has been our tradition from the time of the synagogue and its practice has been revered and renewed in every major period of church history. Taking cues from the Bible and from the way in which Jesus taught, preachers can tell stories. They can use narrative, drama, symbols, and present vivid images. They can use examples from life and about persons. In many ways a preacher can capture the attention and imagination of children in the congregation. Not that children will hear and understand all seventeen or twenty minutes of a sermon—few adults do either—but there is the likely possibility that children will understand a point, be stimulated by a story or example, and will carry an image in their minds that will eventuate into a fully developed theological concept.

Preaching that speaks to children as well as adults is not an untried, impossible art. At the end of this chapter is an article, "The Word of God for the Whole Congregation," (Appendix A) and a collection of excerpts from sermons by the Rev. Walter B. Funk and the Rev. Davis Thomas (Appendix B). Notice how references to the interests and activities of children are woven into the fabric of the sermons. Children listen to the sermons and find themselves caught up in parts of the sermons. They have been addressed and they know that Walter and Davis want them to hear God's Word too.

Davis Thomas and Walter Funk are the first to say that you can do better. The sermon excerpts reflect their styles and personalities and they communicate in the setting of particular congregations. Every preacher needs to do the same work of weaving message, person, congregation, and setting into the marvelous communication which is the sermon.

In every chapter this book has advocated the rights of children to receive ministry, to participate in the total life of the church, and to worship with the congregation. In the end we discover again that when we minister to the child we find that the child has ministered to us.

Appendix A

The Word of God for the Whole Congregation

When the congregation gathers for worship the Word of God is one indispensable element. The people are called to listen obediently to scripture and sermon. Since baptized children are members of the church this summons includes them. Usually, however, scripture is read and sermons are planned with adults in mind. We assume children will gain nothing from this part of our worship, and generally they fulfill our expectations.

With good intentions some pastors and churches offer a substitute judged suitable for children—a children's sermon, an alternate activity outside the sanctuary where noise and motion are acceptable, or a crossword puzzle or paper work to occupy them in the sanctuary. No matter what good motives prompt us to exclude children from scripture and sermon, the action remains a form of discrimination and deprivation.

No pastor would summon everyone over forty to gather around the pulpit every Sunday for a special message. What church has a policy of dismissing every adult from the sanctuary who does not seem likely to have undivided attention and total comprehension? What worship committee distributes games in case restless adults disturb those around them?

We need to direct our energy and imagination to speaking God's Word to children rather than devising substitutes for this worship experience. The Word of God—scripture and sermon—can be heard by all ages. Here are some suggestions that may help us reach this goal.

Think positively about inclusive preaching.

Preaching with children in mind is not limiting. They need the gospel in every area of their lives. Virtually any sermon subject suitable for adults is suitable for children if it is appropriately applied. By the time children are six, if not before, they have struggled with fear, guilt, rejection, failure, sorrow, pride, and the use of power—to name only a few. They have felt joy, wonder, awe, and love. Children fear failure in school just as adults fear failure in jobs. Christ's call to trust God's care can be applied to both. The gospel does not need to be edited for children.

Inclusive preaching requires one to be clear, concise, concrete, and vivid—effective characteristics for addressing any age. Reading scripture to children calls for distinct speech, intelligent phrasing, and some explanation of context—no handicaps for any person's listening.

Children do have some specific limitations. Complicated sentence structure, clause piled on clause, quickly loses them. Vocabulary is less of a problem. New words become comprehensible in context if they are used with care. Early elementary children have little sense of history or geography. Since one purpose of preaching is to make the Bible both local and contemporary, dealing with this limitation will only sharpen homiletic skills.

Read the scripture well.

The scripture is not a prelude to the sermon; the sermon is a commentary on the scripture. Bible reading deserves the same attention given sermon delivery. Practice reading scripture in advance. Read poetry as poetry, proclamation with excitement and force, a story with some feel for narrative. Tape record yourself reading Ephesians 1 to get a good perspective on the challenge of "idea" passages.

Find ways to help the congregation see and feel the passage as well as hear it. Where it is appropriate, read the scripture dramatically. Let the conversation between Jesus and the Samaritan woman be a conversation with two readers. Use a variety of voices, including young persons'. *Readers Theatre Comes to Church* (by Gordon Bennett, John Knox Press, 1972) is an excellent guide for this.

Involve the congregation in scripture reading using a method more varied than responsive readings. Many psalms can be read antiphonally. Some scriptures almost call for a congregational voice. (Mark 2:12—"We never saw anything like this!") Pre-service rehearsals of congregational reading are possible.

Instead of a picture of the church for the three-hundredth time, let the bulletin cover be an interpretation of the text drawn by a child, young person, or adult. (Picturing scripture and blocking scripture for dramatic reading have the fringe benefit of being excellent Bible study for any age in the church.)

Set the scripture in context simply and briefly: "This is a letter from a pastor to a quarreling church." "Pilgrims sang this song as they came near to the temple."

Provide pulpit Bibles and bookmarks for children to use. Print the text when you use a different translation. Seeing the scripture helps people "hear" it.

Keep children and their experiences before you as you plan.

Knowing the congregation is one requirement for good preaching. Most ministers are aware of the hopes, joys, tastes, prejudices, problems, and crises that color their adult members' lives. Awareness of children enables a minister to address them in sermons.

Draw up a "life event" chart for children at various ages between 4 and 13. Go through the year as an elementary child—the beginning of school, holidays, tests, school elections, sports competition, and summer vacation. What decisions do they make? What challenges do they face? What abilities do they have? What home crises touch their lives? As you apply scripture remember that the sense of accomplishment which accompanies riding a bicycle the first time may match that felt with a college diploma or a job promotion.

Visit the schools your children attend.

Teach in the church school occasionally to keep the "feel" of children's questions and conversation.

Watch television on Saturday morning, late afternoon, and early evening.

Become familiar with the literature of childhood.

There are several reasons for doing this. One is it will help you understand children—what they like and what they know. Another is this: the style of juvenile literature demonstrates what can be done with simple sentences and limited vocabulary. The quickest way to gain clear information on any subject is to read a book written for an upper elementary age. Beyond this, juvenile literature may be an excellent source of illustrations.

A large body of literature is shared by all ages in the congregation. In one sermon the plight of Humpty Dumpty served to introduce the consequences of sin. In a sermon called "Why Doesn't God Do Something?" the minister began by saying: "Suppose that every time we did something wrong we saw the results right away? When we opened our mouths to gossip out would pop toads and snakes. When we lied our noses would grow an inch!"

There are classics of fantasy that illustrate the Christian life: the Narnia series by C. S. Lewis, the works of George MacDonald (in which the figure of God is always a woman), and Madeline L'Engle's Newberry award winner, *A Wrinkle in Time.*

Contemporary literature known by most school children can serve as well as Shakespeare, Faulkner, and Kafka. Probably every child in the country has read the limited vocabulary book, *Green Eggs and Ham*, a perfect example of prejudice. Maurice Sendak's *Pierre* in the *Nutshell Library* is a model of noninvolvement. Books by E. B. White and Dr. Seuss are other examples of widely popular reading. Juvenile biographies provide illustrations that speak to school age children. Elizabeth Gray's biography of William Penn gives a vivid picture of the cost of discipleship in one young man's life.

An anthology of children's literature, such as Arbuthnot's *Children and Books*, can offer some guidance in reading. School and public librarians can make suggestions. Most schools expose children to all Newberry and Caldecott award winners.

Hearing the Word of God is more than an intellectual activity.

Reformed worship places great emphasis on understanding. Without sacrificing this, we need to remember that understanding is not solely intellectual and that not all learning is verbal. By being with grown-ups who listen with expectancy to God's Word children catch something. Congregational listening is different from private reading or even family devotions. It places us in the community. While there are many things children ignore or do not understand in a specific sermon, one thing they *can* understand is the importance of this act in the lives of the adults and the community they love and trust. This is a cumulative understanding. It does not come from one Sunday in the sanctuary.

Hearing the Word of God is an appropriate challenge for children.

Our society expects children to learn through words by at least the age of six. Law requires them to go to school, to listen, to follow directions, to acquire reading skills, and to increase vocabulary and comprehension. We require them to take initial steps that will make them responsible members of a democratic society. When the church, on the other hand, expects children not to understand words and takes no steps to develop comprehension, the contrast implies something about what we value. The beginning of public education is a reasonable time to include children in the act of listening to God's Word.

Our theology of church membership and worship makes this inclusion of children essential. The impact on the life of the child of the preaching/listening act shared with adults makes sound Christian nurture. And the minister who broadens his or her preaching to speak the Word of God to children will acquire in the process increased homiletic skills.

Virginia Thomas

Appendix B

Examples of Sermons That Reach All Age Groups

Scripture: Deuteronomy 4:1–8; Mark 7:1–8, 14, 15, 21, 23
Sermon: A People of the Law

You must be in bed by 7:30.
Wipe your feet before coming into the house.
Hand in a term paper by December 2 or fail the course.
Don't chew gum in class.
Do not drive over 55 miles per hour.
File your income tax by April 15.
Every person here knows what rules are. And we do not always like them.

We know we must have some rules if people are going to live together. Speed limits, starting times, and deadlines are necessary. Yet we feel they limit us. They take away our freedom and hem us in. We think laws are like fences.

The Bible, however, speaks of God's rules or laws in a different way.

God's laws, of course, are not exactly like the rules of parents, schools, or governments.

Being in bed by 7:30 changes as we grow older.

Being in school by 8:20 may change to noon if double sessions are necessary.

The speed limit may change from 55 to 65.

God's laws are lasting. They apply to every age.

But they are not like fences. They are more like a foundation—like the concrete base on which your house is built. God's laws do not limit us and hem us in. Instead they are a solid rock on which we may build. . . . .

Davis Thomas

Scripture: 1 Timothy 4:11–16; Matthew 28:16–20
Sermon: An Event or a Process?

Do you remember the first day of school?

Whether it was last week or the last century, most of us can still remember the excitement and anticipation.

We prepared for the day long in advance. We laid out clothes and supplies. We checked to find school bus schedules and pickup points. Then the building seemed so big, the halls so long, the room so crowded as we entered our first day of public education.

Then the first day was over.

But was your education complete? Were you through?

Could you say at the end of the second day, "Now I've learned enough?"

Just when do you complete your education? At the end of the first grade? or the sixth grade? or high school? Are you educated when you finish college?

No, the first day of school is not all there is to learning. The first day is an important event, but education is a lifelong process. It is something we may begin on a certain day, but it continues as long as we live.

This helps understand something about salvation and the work of the church. . . .

Davis Thomas

Scripture: Luke 13:1–9
Sermon: Using Up the Ground

Suppose you bought a beautiful new car.

You had always wanted a car that was fire engine red.

You had always wanted a big luxury car, too.

So, in spite of the high cost of gasoline, you decided to splurge and get a Cadillac.

It had red and white leather seats, a plush red carpet on the floor. It had air conditioning, power steering, power brakes, and reclining seats.

It had everything you had ever dreamed of in a car, except wheels. It had no wheels.

You could go out and sit in it, but you couldn't go anywhere. You could play in it, or sleep in it, or cool yourself in it. But you couldn't take a trip in it.

After a while you begin to think you have made a mistake. It would have been better to have something you could get around in. You need a car for transportation. It would have been better to have bought a car for what a car is really intended to be and do.

You could say of that Cadillac, "It's just using up the ground."

Or you may know a student in an arithmetic class in school. Every day she gets the assignment off the board. And every day the teacher shows how to add, subtract, multiply, or divide. But when you see her paper at the end of the semester, no problems have been worked. The sheets are filled with pictures and designs. They are beautiful. If you saw them you would rave about how well she draws. But she can't do a single arithmetic problem.

She'd missed the whole purpose of the class. She's just been taking up space—or using up the ground.

In a way, this is what the parable today is saying about the fig tree and about life. The fig tree has a purpose—to produce figs. It may give shade, or add beauty to the landscape, but it was planted to produce figs. . . .

Davis Thomas

Scripture: Isaiah 43:18–25; 2 Corinthians 1:18–22; Mark 2:1–12
Sermon: Epiphany VII

. . . We are constantly saying, "Nothing surprises me anymore!" We may be proceeding through our working day. Or we may be riding our bicycles to Woodland Park School. Or we may be reading an assignment in the University library. Whatever we may be doing, something unexpected may happen all of a sudden. But we will tend not to be surprised, pleased, shocked, or excited by it. Whether you are seven years old or eighty-four years old or anywhere in between, for all of us I wish we had the zest for living each moment.

My fifteen-month-old daughter has that zest. Her face and hands and voice are always reacting to surprise and joy. She likes to go to a park near our home each afternoon. Just a few days ago we were down there. She was toddling about, exploring the dirt, leaves, and fountain. I got distracted by watching a "pick-up" football game across the creek. When I looked around my daughter had climbed all the way to the top of the twelve-foot slide. When she saw that I saw her she let out a squeal of surprised joy—joy that her little legs could do such marvelous things. This was a marvelous *epiphany* in her life.

. . . Our confessions affirm that God is with us. And as early as four years old children sing in Sunday church school, "God loves us, God loves us, God loves us, and sent his Son."

Walter B. Funk

Scripture: 2 Chronicles 36:14–21; Ephesians 2:1–10; John
          3:14–21
Sermon: Lent IV

. . . Or we could lift our eyes from that small part of the world and look at a larger slice of the world. That's what a young friend and I did a few days ago. Allen and I were looking at a large map of the United States. Allen was very interested in New York. We looked at that on the map, and then at the states near New York—Pennsylvania, Ohio, and all the way to Illinois. We looked at Utah and then at California on this large map. I commented on each of these areas out of my own experience and Allen asked questions about these places. He told about his own experiences. We had a sense of getting a bigger picture by sharing our experiences together. Together we got a bigger picture than we could have gotten by ourselves.

Walter B. Funk

A Bibliography of Printed Resources on Children and Worship

Although some of these resources are out of print, you may be able to find them in your church or public library.

General Works on Worship

Abba, Raymond. *Principles of Christian Worship.* New York: Oxford University Press, 1957. A concise and sound presentation of the meaning and responses of public worship.

Hoon, Paul W. *The Integrity of Worship.* Nashville: Abingdon Press, 1977. A substantive and balanced presentation of a Protestant theology of worship.

Jansen, John Frederick. *Let Us Worship God: An Interpretation for Families.* Richmond: CLC Press, 1966. This guide for families includes suggestions for involving children in worship and for experiencing and expressing basic elements of Christian life, such as forgiveness. An appendix by the editors provides guidelines for worship in the home.

MacGregor, Geddes. *The Rhythm of God: A Philosophy of Worship.* New York: Seabury Press, 1974. A thought-provoking and gracefully written statement from a sacramental perspective with valuable insights about when to conserve and when to innovate in worship.

Wardlaw, Don M. *Takestock: Worship—A Learning Program About Corporate Christian Worship.* Atlanta: John Knox Press, 1976. This multimedia kit of cassettes, study booklets, filmstrip, and worksheets enables a group to study about worship and then to plan a service. The first session helps participants to share experiences of the sights and sounds of worship.

White, James F. *New Forms of Worship.* Nashville: Abingdon Press, 1971. This is an excellent presentation of the issues at stake in contemporary liturgical renewal. Theologically and historically responsible, this book touches all bases in what is contemporary in worship.

——— *The Worldliness of Worship.* New York: Oxford University Press, 1967. This book seeks primarily to help Christian laity realize their part in a vital aspect of Christianity that is in reformation: worship.

Worship and Nurture

Benson, Dennis C., and Stewart, Stan J. *The Ministry of the Child.* Nashville: Abingdon Press, 1979. Narratives of what children have done, generally in a church setting, lead to comments and questions for discussion on the ways children minister to the rest of us.

Cully, Iris V. *Christian Worship and Church Education.* Philadelphia: Westminster Press, 1967. This is a thorough and informed book. The significance of worship is primary and the educational task of the church is described within that priority. The suggestions are theologically and educationally sound.

Curran, Dolores. *Who, Me Teach My Child Religion?* Minneapolis: Winston Press, 1974. This book provides support and practical advice for parents as they seek to teach religious faith and practice to their children.

Fritz, Dorothy Bertolet. *The Child and the Christian Faith.* Richmond: CLC Press, 1964. Sensible suggestions about how children learn and how they participate in worship are interspersed throughout this book on the church's educational ministry with children.

Koulomzin, Sophie. *Our Church and Our Children.* Crestwood, NY: St. Vladimir's Seminary Press, 1975. Written from an Orthodox Christian perspective, this book offers a healthy balance to Protestant emphases in religious education. The suggestions in this book reflect a good use of current psychological findings and Orthodox Christian appreciation for nurture in the mystery and wholeness of faith.

Neville, Gwen K., and Westerhoff, John H., III. *Learning Through Liturgy.* New York: Seabury Press, 1978. The thesis of this book is that we learn through worship. This concept is spelled out and suggestions are offered for emphasizing the liturgical and ritual life of the church.

Sherrill, Lewis Joseph. *The Rise of Christian Education.* New York: Macmillan Company, 1944. This older book has thorough, useful information on how children were taught religious traditions and worship in Hebrew and early Christian life, particularly in the home.

Sloyan, Virginia, ed. *Liturgy Committee Handbook.* Washington, D.C.: The Liturgical Conference, 1971. This manual is a solid combination of theological and practical information about worship and how it can be planned by members of the congregation.

Sundquist, Ralph R., Jr. *Whom God Chooses: The Child in the Church.* Second edition revised and edited by Jack A. Worthington and W. Ben Lane. Philadelphia: Geneva Press, 1973. The church's ministry with younger children, with concern for how they participate in the life and worship of a congregation.

Weber, Hans-Ruedi. *Jesus and the Children: Biblical Resources for Study and Preaching.* Atlanta: John Knox Press, 1979. Interpretive material and suggestions for teaching and preaching on passages in which Jesus spoke about children are presented in a thought-provoking manner in this book.

Worthington, Jack A. and Vivian R. *Designing Church Education for Children Under Six.* Philadelphia: Geneva Press, 1969. While acknowledging the limitations on the ability of children under six years of age to participate in worship, this booklet offers suggestions for meaningful involvement of young children in worship.

Child Development

Brusselmans, Christiane, with Wakin, Edward. *A Parents' Guide: Religion for Little Children.* Huntington, IN: Our Sunday Visitor Publications, 1970. Practical suggestions to parents are given for family life and activities which enable children to experience religious practice and traditional, common home and church activities. An appendix offers short answers to typical children's questions about religion.

Cully, Iris V. *Christian Child Development.* San Francisco: Harper & Row, 1979. The theories of contemporary psychologists, including Erikson, Piaget, Bruner, and Goldman, are presented and their application for religious education is shown.

Goldman, Ronald. *Readiness for Religion: A Basis for Developmental Education* New York: Seabury Press, 1970. Information about and suggestions for identifying how children think about religious topics and how educators must plan for children's education. This book is a practical follow-up to Goldman's research, reported in *Religious Thinking from Childhood to Adolescence* (Seabury Press, 1968).

Greenleaf, Barbara Kaye. *Children Through the Ages*. New York: McGraw-Hill, 1978. This book is a brief overview of how society has understood and treated children throughout history.

Madge, Violet. *Introducing Young Children to Jesus*. New York: More-house-Barlow Co., 1971. Based on research with children as well as insight from their own questions about Jesus, this book suggests ways to teach children about Jesus, using familiar biblical stories.

Children in Worship

Hilliard, Dick. *The Lord Blesses Me*. Resource Publications (1978), P.O. Box 444, Saratoga, CA 95070. Descriptions of learning centers on greeting, word, praise, creation, sharing, and witness for children and young families.

Matthews, Edward. *Celebrating Mass with Children: A Commentary on the Directory of Masses with Children*. New York: Paulist Press, 1978. This interpretation of the Eucharist shows how children can participate and has application for traditions other than Roman Catholic. Emphasis is on teaching children how to worship.

Pike, Morris D. *All Our Days—Laugh and Praise*. New York: Friendship Press, 1974. Poems, songs, prayers, and interesting methods are given in this book to teach children how to worship. A phonograph record, *Laugh and Praise*, is available as a separate supplement.

———— *Primary Teacher's Guide on "Worship Anytime, Anywhere."* New York: Friendship Press, 1974. This booklet gives ideas for teaching about worship in a Sunday church school setting. The suggestions make use of the book, *All Our Days—Laugh and Praise*.

Rabalais, Maria, and Hall, Howard. *Children, Celebrate—Resources for Youth Liturgy*. New York: Paulist Press, 1974. Resources for worship by children in a Roman Catholic setting, including biblical themes, readings, music, and liturgies, but adaptable for general worship.

Sladen, Kathleen. *Let Them Worship*. Toronto: SKHS Publications,

1976. This is a book of resources for teaching children ages 4 to 12 about worship, including communion.

Sloyan, Virginia, ed. *Signs, Songs, and Stories: Another Look at Children's Liturgies.* Washington, D.C.: The Liturgical Conference, 1974. A successful follow-up to *Children's Liturgies,* with more articles on how children learn, the place of liturgy in the church, and how worship can become more active. The place of stories and storytelling is emphasized.

Sloyan, Virginia, and Huck, Gabe, eds. *Children's Liturgies.* Washington, D.C.: The Liturgical Conference, 1970. This collection of articles is an important breakthrough in the treatment of children and worship. A sympathetic approach to children's capacities and interests is combined with informed understandings of worship. Both traditional and contemporary worship is dealt with; worship is seen as the central act of the church since its beginning, and as an act which must be relevant to the church and its people today. Worship is seen as being active, celebrative, ritualistic, and sacramental.

White, Jack Noble. *Everything You Need for Children's Worship (Except Children).* St. Anthony Messenger Press (1978), 1615 Republic Street, Cincinnati, OH 45210. Formats, ideas, activities, and music for children's worship are provided in this resource.

Woodward, Thomas B. *To Celebrate.* New York: Seabury Press, 1973. Helps for learning and celebrations are suggested for children in home, church school, and congregational settings.

Worship Alive Series. Discipleship Resources, P.O. Box 840, Nashville, TN 37202. This is an ongoing series by the education division of the United Methodist Church. Among the titles concerning children and worship are "Keep Them in Their Place?" by William Willimon, "Take It from the Beginning: Handbook for a Children's Choir Director" by Charlotte Lewis, and "Experiencing Worship with Children" by Elise Shoemaker and Doris Willis.

The Sacraments and Children

Evenson, C. Richard. *God's Table of Grace: Leader's Guide and Learner Book.* Augsburg, Concordia, Fortress Press, 1977. This material for Lutherans is designed for children preparing for the Lord's

Supper with the help of their parents. Its suggestions are useful for any tradition.

Hines, John M. *By Water and the Holy Spirit: New Concepts of Baptism, Confirmation, and Communion.* New York: Seabury Press, 1973. Intended as a help for Episcopalians facing the need to integrate children into the worship life of the church because of certain worship reforms, this small book has useful understandings of how children learn and how the liturgy serves all members of the church, including children.

Holmes, Urban T., III. *Young Children and the Eucharist.* New York: Seabury Press, 1972. This short book is significant not only for its theological and historical understandings of worship and the sacraments but also for its application of educational and psychological insights. Holmes has applied the findings of Erikson and Piaget critically and creatively in the areas of religious development and education.

MacNaughton, E. Margaret, ed. *Water, Bread, and Wine.* Philadelphia: Geneva Press, 1975. This booklet is a series of articles on the sacraments and on children and communion. Notable is Horace Allen's article on how to enhance children's participation in a theologically responsible and also practical way.

Roloff, Marvin L., ed. *Welcome to the Lord's Table.* Minneapolis: Augsburg; Philadelphia: Board of Publication, Lutheran Church in America, 1971. This set of materials advocates the celebrating of communion at an early age and provides suggestions for families and congregations for changes in worship practices and for preparing children for communion. Set includes guide for leaders, book for communicants, book for parents, filmstrip, and record.

The Church Year

Alternative Celebrations Catalogue, 1924 East 3rd Street, Bloomington, IN 47401. This publication gives suggestions for planning a variety of celebrations with meaning for all ages. Emphasis is placed on ecologically sound, nonmaterialistic, peace-oriented activities and gifts.

Carson, Mary Faith, and Duba, Arlo D. *Praise God: Worship Through the Year.* General Assembly Mission Board, Presbyterian Church,

U.S. This is the 1979-80 Bible Study Book for the Women of the Church (PCUS). It presents basic understandings of worship and the celebration of the church year. Suggestions for group study are provided.

Cronin, Gaynell Bordes. *Holy Days and Holidays: Prayer Celebrations with Children.* Minneapolis: Winston Press, 1979. Twenty-four holidays and celebrations are presented in this book, such as for Epiphany, Christian Unity Week, Pentecost, Independence Day, All Saints' Day, and St. Nicholas' Day. Symbols, crafts, and liturgies are included.

Griggs, Patricia and Donald. *Generations Learning Together.* Nashville: Abingdon Press, 1976. Practical suggestions are provided for intergenerational groups to prepare for communion, Advent, Christmas, Easter, and Pentecost.

——— *Teaching and Celebrating Advent.* Nashville: Abingdon Press, 1975. This useful resource includes learning activities, directions for crafts, worship plans, and a complete list of resources. Also see *Teaching and Celebrating Lent-Easter* by the same authors.

Kleinhans, Theodore J., *The Year of the Lord. The Church Year: Its Customs, Growth, and Ceremonies.* St. Louis: Concordia Publishing House, 1967. This concise yet comprehensive book explains the church year and the various elements connected, such as vestments, colors, hymnody, architecture, folklore, and customs.

Rochelle, Jay C. *The Revolutionary Year: Recapturing the Meaning of the Church Year.* Philadelphia: Fortress Press, 1973. This book seeks to show how the liturgical year can be a bridge between the historical and rational background and the existential and mystical side of faith. Examples are given of contemporary ways to celebrate church festivals and seasons.

Russell, Joseph P. *Sharing Our Biblical Story.* Minneapolis: Winston Press, 1979. This book is a full description of how one congregation used the lectionary as the basis for worship and education throughout the church program. Helpful insights are given concerning the use of biblical stories with all ages.

Williams, Doris, and Griggs, Patricia. *Preparing for the Messiah.* Nashville: Abingdon Press, 1977. Helpful insights are offered on the value of church traditions and the celebration of the church year. The major portion of this book gives specific instructions for activities for children and youth to learn about and participate in celebrations of church tradition and the church year.

Drama and Music in Worship with Children

Bennett, Gordon C. *Readers Theatre Comes to Church*. Atlanta: John Knox Press, 1972. Two chapters of this general introduction deal with reading scripture as drama and are valuable resources for adding vitality to the reading of scripture in public worship.

Hudson, Leonora Pirret. *Worship and the Arts*. The Joint Office of Worship of the UPCUSA and PCUS, 1978. This is a set of multimedia kits for studies about "Sounding Praise," "Sharing the Spirit in Music," "Drama in Worship," "Architecture and Worship," "Liturgical Dance," and a sixth kit to use in an actual service of worship.

Peebles, Sue, and Herder, Margaret. *Celebrate a Season*. Choristers Guild, P.O. Box 38188, Dallas, TX 75238. This choir booklet for junior choirs explores three major areas of worship: preparation, proclamation, and dedication, using examples from the seasons of the church year. This is a fine approach to teaching children about worship.

The Choristers Guild is a source for many aids in teaching about worship. Their catalog lists hymn study guides, posters, banner-making guides, and puzzles and games. Their resources include *The End the Beginning* and *An Introduction to Christian Symbolism*.

Ingram, Madeline. *Organizing and Directing Children's Choirs*. Nashville: Abingdon Press, 1959. This probably is the most helpful volume a volunteer director can own.

Jacobs, Ruth K., compiler. *The Children's Choir*, Vol. I. Rock Island, IL: Augustana Press, 1958. Tufts, Nancy Poore. *The Children's Choir*, Vol. II. Philadelphia: Fortress Press, 1965. These two volumes are compilations of articles from the Choristers Guild Letters. The suggestions deal with music and worship education.

Lovelace, Austin C., and Rice, William C. *Music and Worship in the Church*. Nashville: Abingdon Press, 1976. This book is a comprehensive approach to church music, beginning with worship and including administration and planning, choirs, soloists, repertoire, director, organist, and congregation. The bibliography is especially good. See also *The Youth Choir* by the same authors.

Millar, Patrick. *The Story of the Church's Song*. Richmond: John Knox Press, 1962. This brief history will enrich hymnbook use.

Smith, Judy Gattis. *Teaching with Music Through the Church Year*. Nashville: Abingdon Press, 1976. This is a book for the church school to enrich worship through the use of its study suggestions for many situations and ages.

Notes

1. John Calvin, *Institutes of the Christian Religion*, ed. John T. Mc-Neill, trans. Ford Lewis Battles (Philadelphia: Westminster Press, 1960), Book IV: XIV, 6, p. 1281.

2. Erik Erikson first described his understandings of the "Eight Ages of Man" in *Childhood and Society* (New York: W. W. Norton, 1950, 1963).

3. Jean Piaget has written extensively and usually in technical fashion. Those who wish an introduction to his work could consult such books as *Piaget's Theory of Cognitive Development: An Introduction for Students of Psychology and Education*, by Barry J. Wadsworth (New York: David McKay, 1971), or *Children and Adolescents: Interpretive Essays on Jean Piaget*, by David Elkind (New York: Oxford University Press, 1970).

4. Robert W. Hovda, "Familiar Rites and Deeds," in *Children's Liturgies*, ed. Virginia Sloyan and Gabe Huck (Washington, D.C.: The Liturgical Conference, 1970), p. 52.

5. John M. Hines, *By Water and the Holy Spirit: New Concepts of Baptism, Confirmation, and Communion* (New York: Seabury Press, 1973), pp. 64-65, 28-29.

6. Urban T. Holmes III, *Young Children and the Eucharist* (New York: Seabury Press, 1972), p. 58. In his chapter, "A Theology of the Holy Communion," Holmes presents his understanding of how persons perceive, and how symbols are formed and are understood. Holmes claims that symbols can be perceived in ways that do not require an intellect which can reason.

7. Ibid., pp. 59-65.

8. Lewis J. Sherrill, *The Rise of Christian Education* (New York: Macmillan, 1944), p. 25.

9. Joseph A. Grassi, *Jesus as Teacher* (Winona, MN: St. Mary's College Press, 1978), p. 12.

10. Brevard S. Childs, *Memory and Tradition in Israel* (Naperville, IL: Alec R. Allenson, 1962), p. 47.

11. Sherrill, *Christian Education*, p. 48.

12. Ibid., p. 45.

13. Arlo Duba, "Seminarians Who Have Never Been to Church," *Monday Morning,* 3 December 1979, pp. 10-11.

14. Ibid., p. 10.

15. Ibid., pp. 10, 11.

16. These resources are part of the Covenant Life Curriculum used by five denominations, including the Presbyterian Church, U. S., several years ago.

17. Madeline D. Ingram, *Organizing and Directing Children's Choirs* (Nashville: Abingdon Press, 1959), p. 12.